A T H E I S M

THE BASICS

: *The Basics* is a concise and engaging introduction to belief
on-existence of deities. Atheism has long fascinated people
ate around this controversial position may seem daunting.
lively and lucid book, Graham Oppy addresses the follow-
ortant questions:

- t does it mean to be an atheist?
- at is the difference between atheism, agnosticism, theism
- nnocence?
- has atheism been distributed over time and place?
- t does science tell us about atheism?
- there good reasons to be an atheist?
- there good reasons not to be an atheist?
- t do we mean by 'new atheism'?

ı glossary of key terms and suggestions for further reading
ıut, the book considers key philosophical arguments
ıtheism, making this an ideal starting point for anyone
a full introduction to the arguments between those who
ıeistic beliefs and those who do not.

n Oppy is Professor of Philosophy at Monash University,
ıa.

The Basics

Other titles in the series can be found at: https://www.routledge.com/The-Basics/book-series/B

ATHEISM

THE BASICS

Graham Oppy

LONDON AND NEW YORK

First published 2019
by Routledge
2 Park Square, Milton Park, Abingdon, Oxon OX14 4RN

and by Routledge
711 Third Avenue, New York, NY 10017

Routledge is an imprint of the Taylor & Francis Group, an informa business

© 2019 Graham Oppy

British Library Cataloguing in Publication Data
A catalogue record for this book is available from the British Library

Library of Congress Cataloging in Publication Data
Names: Oppy, Graham, 1960- author.
Title: Atheism : the basics / Graham Oppy.
Description: 1 [edition].. | New York : Routledge, 2018. |
Series: The basics | Includes bibliographical references and index.
Identifiers: LCCN 2018018350| ISBN 9781138506916 (hardback : alk. paper) |
ISBN 9781138506961 (pbk. : alk. paper) | ISBN 9781315150383 (ebook)
Subjects: LCSH: Atheism.
Classification: LCC BL2747.3 .O56 2018 | DDC 211/.8--dc23
LC record available at https://lccn.loc.gov/2018018350

ISBN: 978-1-138-50691-6 (hbk)
ISBN: 978-1-138-50696-1 (pbk)
ISBN: 978-1-315-15038-3 (ebk)

Typeset in Bembo
by Taylor & Francis Books

CONTENTS

TABLES

ACKNOWLEDGMENTS

This book is for my atheist friends and colleagues.

I am bound to forget people, but, among those who should be included, there are: Dirk Baltzly, John Bigelow, Russell Blackford, Warren Bonett, Stuart Brock, Greg Dawes, Evan Fales, Steve Gardner, Al Hàjek, Alan Hazen, Jakob Hohwy, Frank Jackson, Lindsay Kleeman, Justin Oakley, Graham Priest, Rob Simpson, Michael Smith, Rob Sparrow, Konrad Talmont-Kaminski and Brian Weatherson.

Thank you one and all (including those I have forgotten to name).

HITCHING A RIDE WITH ARTHUR DENT

Whether or not this work contains any glaring—or perhaps even fatal—inaccuracies, it ought to have the words DON'T PANIC in large, friendly letters on the cover. Yes, this is a book about atheism and atheists, but, no, there is no reason to be fearful of its contents. Indeed, if we were to engage in ferocious editing of its contents, we could probably boil them down to the following simple message: MOSTLY HARMLESS.

The plan of the book is very simple. There are six substantive chapters, each of which addresses a different topic. We begin by distinguishing atheism from the many things with which it is often conflated. Next, we consider the lives of a dozen different atheists from very different times and places. Then we consider what the social sciences tell us about atheists. With this material behind us, we turn to consider a vast range of objections to atheism. After that, we consider what kinds of things might be said on behalf of atheism. Finally, we wind up with some speculation about what the future of atheism might be.

Chapter 2—'Setting the record straight'—explains what I do, and don't, mean by 'atheism'. On my account, 'atheism', 'theism', 'agnosticism', and 'innocence' are all defined in terms of the claim that there are no gods, where 'god' is itself defined (very roughly) in terms of having and exercising top-level power. The definition of these four related terms says nothing about the *strength* or *robustness* of belief, or about the *level of interest* in what is believed, or about whether what is believed is considered to be a *desirable* state of affairs, or about whether it is taken to be important what *other* people believe about the existence of gods, or about how the *intellectual merits* of those who hold dissenting beliefs should be esteemed, or about claims to *proof*, or about claims to *knowledge*. While there are many other terms and distinctions in play in the literature, I find no use for 'weak atheism', 'strong atheism', 'igtheism', 'apatheism', and the like. Accepting that *religion* requires communal displays of costly commitments that enable mastery of existential anxieties, I argue that there can be—and are—religious atheists, but there is no serious prospect of developing artificial 'religions of humanity'.

Chapter 3—'Snapshots from history'—briefly describes the lives and times of twelve atheists, or alleged atheists, from very different times and places: Ajita Kesakambali, Diagoras of Melos, Wang Chong, Abu al-ʿAlaʾ al-Maʿarri, Jean Meslier, Paul Henri d'Holbach, Mary Ann Evans, Emma Goldman, Eric Blair, Margaret Kennedy, Maryam Namazie, and Agomo Atambire. The selection of atheists to discuss in this chapter is arbitrary; there are thousands of atheists who have contributed to the development of atheism while leading interesting lives. However, the selection does convey something of the diversity of atheists across a whole range of dimensions while also filling in some of the historical background to the emergence of atheism as a serious intellectual standpoint.

Chapter 4—'Facts and figures'—considers what the social sciences tell us about atheism and atheists. We begin with a discussion of numbers, noting various difficulties that impede attempts to estimate how many atheists there are, or were, in given populations. We then turn to the use of social scientific data in the assessment of stereotypical beliefs about atheists; for example, that atheists are untrustworthy, law-breaking, immoral, nihilistic, selfish, unhappy, emotionally unstable, mentally deficient, sexually deviant, physically unhealthy and possessed of low life expectancy. We conclude that, to the extent that we can find it, relevant social scientific data do not bear out any of these stereotypes. Moreover, when we look at further social scientific data that is relevant to the profiling of atheists, we find that it suggests that atheists may enjoy some advantages relative to total populations.

Chapter 5—'Common complaints'—canvasses a wide range of objections to atheism: that atheists are fundamentalists; that atheists are political ideologues; that atheists hate gods; that atheism is just another religion; that atheists are anti-religion; that atheists are immoral; that atheists are ignorant; that atheists are horrible; that atheism is unliveable; and that atheism is irrational. Some of the discussion in this chapter draws on the social scientific data discussed in the preceding chapter; much of it is framed in more normative terms. The final part of the discussion—on the question of whether atheism is irrational—discusses arguments for the existence of gods, and considers the prospects for convicting atheists of logical, or evidential, or prudential lapses from intellectual grace.

Chapter 6—'Reasons and arguments'—surveys five types of claims that have been made on behalf of atheism: (a) that atheism is the default position; (b) that stating that there are gods is meaningless or logically inconsistent; (c) that best theistic worldviews are logically inconsistent; (d) that best theistic big pictures are logically inconsistent; and (e) that best theistic big pictures are not as good as best atheistic big pictures. Roughly: a *best theistic big picture* is an idealisation of everything that theists believe that is relevant to their theism, and a *best atheistic big picture* is an idealisation of everything that atheists believe that is relevant to their atheism. Anything that is common to competing best theistic and best atheistic big pictures is *data; best theistic worldviews* and *best atheistic worldviews* are what you arrive at by omitting data from best theistic and best atheistic big pictures. So, even more roughly, (c) claims that theistic theories are 'internally' inconsistent; (d) claims that theistic theories are inconsistent with data; and (e) claims that atheistic theories make a more virtuous fit with data than theistic theories. I argue that there is good reason to *deny* that atheism is the default position, that the claim that there are gods is meaningless or logically inconsistent, that best theistic worldviews are logically inconsistent, and that best theistic big pictures are logically inconsistent. Moreover, I argue that it is ultimately a matter for judgment whether best atheistic big pictures are more theoretically virtuous than best theistic big pictures: this is something about which thoughtful, reflective, intelligent, well-informed people can only agree to disagree.

Chapter 7—'On the road again'—examines the future prospects for atheism. First, I consider—and reject—the suggestion that the rise of 'new' atheism is a straw in the wind suggesting that atheism is on the rise. Next, I consider—and reject—the claims of some philosophers, theologians and sociologists that we currently have good empirical and theoretical reasons for thinking that atheism is in terminal decline. Finally, I make some observations about just how hard it is to provide accurate predictions about the large-scale future of humanity.

While the book is designed to be read from beginning to end, readers might choose to begin with almost any of the chapters. The one caution that I will give is that I suspect that Chapter 6 is harder to come to grips with than the other chapters. If you are not particularly interested in arguments about the existence of God, then you might do better to *omit* Chapter 6 from your first reading of this book. (A similar caution is in place for §5.10 of Chapter 5, and in particular for §5.10.2 within it.)

Apart from the substantive chapters, this book also includes a guide to further reading, a glossary of key terms, and a bibliography.

2

SETTING THE RECORD STRAIGHT

In this chapter, I say what atheism is, and what it is not. Different people have very different conceptions of atheism, and they make very different identifications of atheism with things from which it should be carefully distinguished. Here are some things that people have said about atheism that you might like to think about before you proceed to hear what I have to say on the matter:

> We are all atheists about most of the gods that humanity has ever believed in. Some of us just go one god further.
>
> (Dawkins 2004: 150)

> To say that atheism is not a religion is the equivalent of saying that anarchy is not really a political creed.
>
> (Jinn 2013: 311)

> All children are atheists, they have no idea of God.
>
> (Holbach 1772/1900: paragraph 30)

> Atheism is the philosophical equivalent of a fish denying the existence of land because he lacks the means to experience it.
>
> (Snyder undated)

I will return to these quotations at the end of this chapter. (No peeking ahead!)

2.1 *ATHEISTS AND ATHEISM*

Not everyone uses the words 'atheism' and 'atheist' in the way that I do. According to the way that I use these words, **atheism** is the claim that there are no gods, and **atheists** are those who believe that there are no gods.

Given the way that I use these words, I maintain that it is true that atheists also fail to believe that there are gods. However, there are at least two other groups of people who fail to believe that there are gods.

First, there are what I shall call '**innocents**': those who have never considered the question whether there are gods and who, for this reason, have no opinion on the matter. Typically, innocents are those who do not possess the concept of *god*; they are not able to form the thought that there are gods. Examples of innocents include: infants, those with advanced Alzheimer's, adults who never acquire the concept of *god*, and so forth. In all of these cases, there is failure to believe that there are gods but not atheism.

Second, there are **agnostics**: people who have considered the question of whether there are gods but have suspended judgment, neither believing that there are no gods nor believing that there is at least one god. While atheists and agnostics (and innocents) are alike in failing to believe that there are gods, atheists are distinguished from agnostics (and innocents) in believing that there are no gods.

Given that **theists** are those who believe that there is at least one god, we have a nice fourfold distinction among beings that are capable of having beliefs: at any given time, each of these beings is either an atheist, or an agnostic, or an innocent, or a theist, and none of these beings falls into more than one of these categories. Perhaps you might think that there is room for a fifth category: benighted beings who believe both that there are no gods and that there is at least one god. It is not clear to me that there could be such beings. Even if there can be such beings, they have no role to play in the further discussion in this book. Perhaps you might think that there can be borderline cases where it just isn't clear whether someone does or does not believe that there are no gods; at worst, borderline cases add an oft-seen level of complexity to the fourfold distinction.

This nice fourfold distinction is a very recent achievement. There is no widely established use of the word 'innocent' for those who have never considered the question whether there are gods, and the word 'agnostic' was only introduced into the English language by Thomas Huxley in the second half of the nineteenth century. Moreover, the virtues of adoption of this nice fourfold distinction are obscured by the long history of pejorative use of the terms 'atheism' and 'atheist'. For as far back as we have written records, there is a history of persecution of 'atheists' (as there is of 'apostates', 'blasphemers', 'heretics', and the like). Denial of the existence of gods worshipped in particular places at particular times often attracted charges of 'atheism' despite the fact that those at whom the charges were levelled believed in other gods. For example, many Romans called early Christians 'atheists' because those Christians denied the existence of the Roman gods; and, in the later stages of the empire, many Christians called pagans 'atheists' because those pagans denied the existence of the Christian God.

It is clear that we *could* endorse context-sensitive uses of the terms 'atheist' and 'atheism' that fit historical usage: we could say that, from the standpoint of the Romans, Christians are atheists, and that, from the standpoint of the Christians, Romans are atheists, and so on. But this is all just needless prolixity. Christians and Romans alike believe that there is at least one god; what they disagree about is which gods there are. On the other hand, there are those who claim that there are no gods; those are the people who genuinely deserve the label 'atheist'.

2.2 GODS

My characterisation of 'atheism' and 'atheist' refers to *gods*. What are they? As is almost always the case, it is easiest to give examples: Allah, Baiame, Cheonjiwang, Dagda, Eledumare, Freya, Guta, Horus, Ishara, Julunggul, Kāne, Lir, Minerva, Nabia, Omoikane, Pundjel, Quetzalcoatl, Ra, Shiva, Tengri, Ukko, Vesta, Wiraqucha, Xolotl, Yahweh, and Zeus. Gods are the kinds of things that can properly be added to this list.

Here is a rough attempt at something more like a traditional definition: **gods** are sufficiently highly ranked supernatural beings who have and exercise power over the natural universe. This attempt is rough not least because 'sufficiently highly ranked' is vague. In many pantheons, there are major gods, minor gods, and ranges of lesser entities that may or may not properly be called 'gods'.

Theists—those who believe that there is at least one god— divide into two classes. **Polytheists** believe that there is more than one god. **Monotheists** believe that there is exactly one god. Typically, monotheists are happy to call the one god in which they believe 'God', though they very often have other names for it as well. Some monotheists object to the suggestion that God is a god, typically on the grounds that their God uniquely resists categorisation. Since these monotheists affirm that God has and exercises power over the natural universe and is not under the power of any more highly ranked being, it is hard to see why they baulk at the claim that God is a god. But, in any case, we could adjust our definitions to fit their whim: monotheists believe either that God exists, or that there is exactly one god, and atheists believe that there are no gods and that God does not exist. In the interests of brevity, I shall stick with the simpler formulations that I gave initially; those who need them can take the adjustments as read.

2.3 MODES OF BELIEF

My characterisation of 'atheists' says nothing about the strength or robustness of atheistic belief.

Sometimes, we think of belief as an **all-or-nothing** affair: for any given claim, either you believe that claim, or you believe the negation of that claim, or you suspend judgment between the claim and the negation of the claim, or you have never paid any attention to the claim. When we introduced our fourfold distinction, we were thinking about belief in this all-or-nothing way: given the claim that there are no gods, either you are an atheist who believes this claim, or you are a theist who believes the negation of this claim, or you are an agnostic who suspends judgment about this claim, or you are an innocent who has never paid any attention to this claim.

That we think about belief in this all-or-nothing way does not prevent us from drawing distinctions between different ways in which beliefs can be held. Even though belief is all-or-nothing, beliefs can be held with different kinds of conviction: some atheists are certain that there are no gods; some atheists are very strongly persuaded that there are no gods; some atheists are fairly sure that there are no gods; some atheists are only slightly swayed in favour of there being no gods; and so on. Moreover, even though belief is all-or-nothing, beliefs can be held with different levels of resistance to revision: for some atheists, the belief that there are no gods is unshakeable; for some atheists, the belief that there are no gods is not so deeply rusted on that it could not be given up; for some atheists, the belief that there is no god is one that they might readily lose; and so forth. The two scales that we have just introduced—*strength* and *resilience*—are largely independent: an atheist could be currently certain that there are no gods while nonetheless being quite open to giving up the belief; and an atheist could currently be only slightly swayed in favour of there being no gods while also having no inclination to move away from *that* position.

Sometimes, we think of belief in terms of **credences**: for any given claim, you assign some probability to that claim. When we think of beliefs as credences, we suppose that, if you assign probability p to a claim, then you (ought to) assign probability $1 - p$ to the negation of that claim. If an atheist assigns a credence of 0.85 to the claim that there are no gods, then that atheist assigns a credence of 0.15 to the claim that there is at least one god. On the assumption that credences are best represented by single probabilities, an atheist will have a credence that falls somewhere in the interval that is greater than 0.5 and no greater than 1. While there is some loose correspondence between these credences and what we called 'strength' in the case of all-or-nothing belief, there is no straightforward mapping from belief as credence to all-or-nothing belief. Most of the following discussion will be framed in terms of all-or-nothing belief.

2.4 *OTHER ATTITUDES*

Belief is not the only attitude that can be taken up towards claims. While atheists are united in *believing* that there are no gods, atheists differ in other attitudes that they take towards the claim that there are no gods.

Some atheists are deeply *interested* in the claim that there are no gods: some atheists devote their lives to investigating this claim, and to arguing about it with theists and agnostics. Other atheists have little or no interest in the claim that there are no gods; having reached the view that there are no gods, these atheists turn their attention to other matters, steering clear of controversies that arise in connection with the claim that there are no gods. And, of course, other atheists fall somewhere on the spectrum that lies between the two positions just mentioned.

Some atheists *want* it to be the case that there are gods. Often enough, these atheists want it to be the case that there are particular gods. Many atheists who were previously theists regret their loss of belief; they would like it to be the case that the gods in which they once believed exist. However, there are atheists who want it to be the case that there are no gods; these atheists typically suppose that the value of our existence—and the value of the universe in which we exist—would be diminished if there were gods. And there are atheists who occupy intermediate positions: for example, there are atheists who simply do not give a fig whether there are certain kinds of gods. (Plausibly, more or less everyone would want it to be the case that particular gods do not exist. Surely very few people *want* it to be the case that Adro, Ahriman, Batara Kala, Coatlicue, Cronobog, Elrik, Hel, Sedna, and Sekhmet exist.)

Some atheists *care* about the attitudes that other people take towards the claim that there are no gods. Often enough, these atheists think that it is bad that there are people who believe that there are gods. Sometimes, though, atheists who care about the attitudes that other people take towards the claim that there are no gods suppose that it is good that there are people who believe that there are gods. Many freethinkers in the eighteenth and nineteenth centuries thought that belief in gods serves important social functions that might be lost if no one believed in gods. It is not a forgone conclusion that you want everyone else to share the beliefs that you hold.

Some atheists suppose that all thoughtful, reflective, sufficiently intelligent, sufficiently well-informed people who give serious attention to the matter believe that there are no gods. That is, some atheists suppose that those who do not believe that there are no gods are *thoughtless*, or *stupid*, or *ignorant*, or perhaps all three together. (It takes no effort to find atheist memes with tags like the following: 'The human brain is an amazing organ. It keeps on working 24 hours a day, 7 days a week, and 52 weeks a year, from before you leave the womb, right up until you find God.' 'If you could reason with theists there would be no theists.' 'The lions generally did not like eating monotheists because they were so full of shit.' 'Aren't you a little too old for an imaginary friend?' Etc.) Other atheists suppose that there are thoughtful, reflective, sufficiently intelligent, sufficiently well-informed people who give serious attention to the matter who fail to believe that there are no gods. These atheists suppose that there can be reasonable disagreement, between thoughtful, reflective, sufficiently intelligent, sufficiently well-informed people, about the existence of gods. Given that there are hundreds of millions of atheists in the world, it should not be the least bit surprising that, while *some* of them are bellicose, bigoted, churlish, cocksure, flippant, graceless, phoney, pretentious, rancorous, smug, spiteful, vain, and so on, there are many atheists who are none of these things.

2.5 *PROOF AND KNOWLEDGE*

Some people suppose that one does not count as an atheist merely because one believes that there are no gods; rather, in order to count as an atheist, one must further suppose that one has *proof* that there are no gods, or that one *knows* that there are no gods, or that one is *certain* that there are no gods. I take it that all of these views are mistaken. True enough, there are some atheists who claim to have proofs that there are no gods; and there are some atheists who think that they are required to make the further claim that they know that there are no gods; and there are some atheists who are certain that there are no gods. But there are many atheists who deny that they have proofs that there are no gods; and there are many atheists who deny that they need to make the further claim that they know that there are no gods; and there are many atheists who do not claim to be certain that there are no gods.

The natural home of proof is the formal sciences: mathematics, logic, statistics, game theory, and the like. There are two features that are required in order for derivations to be proofs. First, each of the inferential steps in the derivation should be universally approved by experts. Where this condition is satisfied, there is universal expert agreement that the conclusion of the derivation follows from the premises (i.e. from the claims that were assumed without argument as the starting point of the derivation). Second, each of the premises of the derivation should itself be universally accepted by experts. Where this second condition is not satisfied, in circumstances in which the first condition is satisfied, we do not have a proof of the conclusion of the derivation; rather, we have merely a proof that the conclusion of the derivation follows from the premises. While there are many sets of premises that entail that there are no gods (i.e. while there are many proofs that the claim that there are no gods follows from particular sets of premises), there is no set of premises, on which there is universal expert agreement, that entails that there are no gods. Atheists who suppose that there are derivations of the claim that there are no gods from premises on which there is universal expert agreement are simply mistaken.

Perhaps it might be said that atheists are required to have proofs in the weaker sense: they are required to have derivations of the claim that there are no gods from premises that they accept (even though there is not universal expert agreement on those premises). But it is uncontroversial that any atheist with sufficient time and expertise could construct an endless supply of derivations of the claim that there are no gods from premises that they accept. Consider:

1 If causal reality contains none but natural causal entities with none but natural causal powers, then there are no gods. (Premise.)
2 Causal reality contains none but natural causal entities with none but natural causal powers. (Premise.)
3 (Therefore) There are no gods. (From 1 and 2.)

While the second premise here is controversial, there are many atheists who accept both of these premises. Those atheists will quite properly judge that this argument is sound. But neither the availability of this derivation nor its actual construction does anything to justify the position of those atheists who accept both of the premises. No matter what view you hold about the claim that there are no gods, you will be able to construct arguments like this one that have your view as their conclusion.

Claims to knowledge seem to be stronger than claims to mere belief. I am sure that, among the things that I believe, there are some falsehoods. (It would take an appalling lack of doxastic humility to suppose otherwise!) But one cannot possibly know falsehoods. So, among the things that I believe, there are things that I do not know. But consider some particular claim that I believe—for example, that there are no gods. Can I coherently maintain that I do not know that there are no gods while continuing to maintain that I believe that there are no gods? That seems to depend upon what I take to be required for knowledge. If I think that knowledge requires a high level of confidence— perhaps even certainty—then, if I have a sufficiently low level of confidence in my belief that there are no gods, it seems that I can coherently maintain that I believe, but do not know, that there are no gods. However, if I think that knowledge is merely warranted true belief—and so compatible with any level of confidence that suffices for belief—then it seems that my supposing that I do not know that there are no gods will require my not believing that there are no gods. For, if I suppose that I do not know that there are no gods, then either I am supposing that it is not true that there are no gods, or I am supposing that I am not warranted in believing that there are no gods; and yet I cannot coherently continue to believe that there are no gods while supposing either of these things. (As G. E. Moore pointed out many years ago, there is something paradoxical in one's saying: *there are gods but I believe that there are no gods*; and it seems no better if one says: *there are no gods, but I have no warrant for saying so*.)

Earlier—in §2.3—I noted that atheists do not need to claim to be certain that there are no gods. If we suppose that knowledge requires certainty, then it is clearly not a requirement on atheists that, apart from believing that there are no gods, atheists must take themselves to know that there are no gods. And, if we suppose that knowledge merely requires warranted true belief, then the fact that atheists believe that there are no gods already commits them to supposing that they know that there are no gods. (In the second case, it doesn't follow that atheists should *claim* to know that there are no gods, at least in the company of those who disagree with them on this point. Given that I know that you disagree with me, I can signal my recognition of this disagreement by saying that I *believe* that there are no gods. Before I speak, I know that each of us thinks that the other is mistaken. Claiming to *know* that there are no gods, in these circumstances, would be looking to pick a fight.)

2.6 *OTHER THEORETICAL POSITIONS*

There are many theoretical positions that are routinely conflated with atheism. Some suppose that all atheists are *materialists*. Some suppose that all atheists are *naturalists*. Some suppose that all atheists are *physicalists*. Some suppose that all atheists are *sceptics*. Some suppose that all atheists are *nihilists*. Some suppose that all atheists are *humanists*. All of these identifications are mistaken. It is true that some atheists are materialists, and some atheists are naturalists, and some atheists are physicalists, and some atheists are sceptics, and some atheists are nihilists, and some atheists are humanists. But it is also true that some atheists are not materialists, and some atheists are not naturalists, and some atheists are not physicalists, and some atheists are not sceptics, and some atheists are not nihilists, and some atheists are not humanists.

At least roughly: (1) **materialists** believe that there are none but material entities with none but material causal powers and that well-established science is the touchstone for identifying causal entities and causal powers; (2) **physicalists** believe that there are none but physical entities with none but physical causal powers and that well-established science is the touchstone for identifying causal entities and causal powers; and (3) **naturalists** believe that there are none but natural entities with none but natural causal powers and that well-established science is the touchstone for identifying causal entities and causal powers. These three positions—materialism, physicalism and naturalism—have much in common. Each grants special significance to expert scientific consensus; each makes a controversial claim about the fundamental constituents of the causal order. In line with then current physics, seventeenth century materialists supposed that the fundamental constituents of the causal order are material atoms that interact through contact. In line with contemporary physics, physicalists suppose that the fundamental constituents of the causal order are fundamental physical entities—fundamental physical particles, or fundamental physical fields distributed over a manifold, or the like—with fundamental physical properties that figure in fundamental conservation laws. In line with contemporary natural science, naturalists suppose that the fundamental constituents of the causal order are fundamental natural entities with fundamental natural properties that figure in fundamental natural laws. Given that gods do not have material, or physical, or natural constitutions, these positions are all atheistic. But there are atheists who embrace none of these positions; there are atheists who suppose that there are non-material, non-physical, non-natural causal entities, with non-material, non-physical, non-natural causal properties, none of which are gods.

At least roughly, **sceptics** claim that there is very little that we are rationally justified in believing. In particular, sceptics claim that there is very little that we are rationally justified in believing about the external world, other minds, the extent of the past, morality, modality, meaning, and so forth. Given that sceptics maintain that there is very little that we are rationally justified in believing, it is unsurprising that sceptics typically maintain that we are rationally required to suspend judgment about almost everything. For example, it is characteristic of sceptics to suspend judgment on the question whether there are fairies: if I'm not sure whether there are trees, cars, and other people, then it is hard to see what grounds I could have for being sure that there are no fairies. So it is unsurprising that most atheists are not sceptics: most atheists think that we typically have lots of rationally justified beliefs about the external world, other minds, the extent of the past, morality, modality, meaning, and so on, and most atheists believe that there are no fairies.

At least roughly, **nihilists** either claim that nothing has any value or else suspend judgment on the question whether there is anything that has any value. According to nihilists, either there isn't anything that is right, wrong, good, or bad, or else it is unclear whether there is something that is right, wrong, good, or bad. There are many atheists who are not nihilists; there are many atheists who think that it is: *wrong* to torture small furry animals;

bad that 1% of the world's population holds more than 50% of the world's wealth; *right* that paedophile priests are now being given lengthy gaol terms; and *good* to permit adults to marry their partners of choice. While there may be significant local differences between the values of atheists and theists, there is no doubt that many atheists have values; and, in a great many cases, atheists and theists have the same values.

At least roughly, **humanists** attach central significance to human understanding, human values and human agency. While all atheists attach much more significance to human understanding, human values and human agency than to divine understanding, divine values and divine agency—there being no such things— there are atheists who do not attach primary significance to human understanding, human values and human agency. In particular, some atheists think that it is unduly chauvinistic or anthropocentric to suppose that humans are the most important things in the universe. Instead, these atheists may attach central importance to *existing* things, or to *living* things, or to *minded* things, or the like. Atheists who attach central importance to existing things, or to living things, or to minded things, or the like, are not humanists.

2.7 *FURTHER DISTINCTIONS?*

Some people distinguish between two different kinds of atheism: *strong* ('hard', 'positive') *atheism* and *weak* ('soft', 'negative') *atheism*. Most often, this distinction turns on whether one believes that there are no gods, or whether one merely fails to believe that there are gods. However, as we noted in §2.1, agnostics and innocents also fail to believe that there are gods. Given that we wish to preserve the standard fourfold distinction of attitudes that can be taken towards particular claims, we should distinguish carefully between those who suspend judgment on the question whether there are no gods and those who have never entertained the thought that there are gods. But, given that we have terms for these two positions, we have no need for a further term, 'weak atheism', that encompasses them both. While we could introduce a further distinction—between, say, 'weak positive atheism' and 'weak negative atheism'—we can already get by with the much shorter and no less informative labels 'agnosticism' and 'innocence'. So, in the interests of economy, we should not endorse *this* distinction between strong atheism and weak atheism, but should rather stick with the fourfold distinction introduced in §2.1.

Our earlier discussion has already made it clear that there are many dimensions along which atheistic belief varies. Atheists differ in the strength of their belief, or in the magnitude of their credence, that there are no gods. Atheists differ in the resilience, or fixity, of their belief or credence that there are no gods. Atheists differ in their degree of interest in the question whether there are gods. Atheists differ in what they want in connection with the existence of gods and in the strength of this wanting. Atheists differ in their assessment of the capacities of those who do not believe that there are no gods. Atheists disagree about whether they have proofs that there are no gods. Atheists disagree about whether they know that there are no gods. Atheists differ in whether they are materialists, or physicalists, or naturalists, or sceptics, or nihilists, or humanists. And so on. Given these dimensions of variation, it is clear that there is no obvious way of constructing a binary distinction between *strong* atheists and *weak* atheists. It may be that, in particular contexts, the modifiers 'strong' and 'weak' can be used to mark a salient distinction from the long list of variations in atheistic belief. But there is neither prospect of success nor point in stipulating some further, context-independent assignment of these modifiers.

Some people say that, because the word 'god' is meaningless, it is meaningless to claim that there are no gods. Often enough, people who say that it is meaningless to claim that there are no gods are then uncertain whether they are atheists. At least some suggest that there is a distinctive position—**'igtheism'**—that is occupied by those who say that it is meaningless to claim that there are no gods. It is unclear exactly what is meant by those who say that the word 'god' is meaningless, particularly given that they allow that it is not meaningless to say that it is meaningless to claim that there are no gods. If we can use the word 'god' in sentences that make meaningful claims—as, for example, it seems that we also do when we say that atheists deny that there are gods or that few people suppose that, if there are gods, then Sekhmet is one of them—then why not suppose that the alleged sense in which the word 'god' is meaningless supports and justifies the claim that there are no gods? When A. J. Ayer introduced the proposal that the word 'god' is meaningless—in his classic exposition of logical positivism, *Language Truth and Logic* (Ayer 1936)—he claimed that the resulting position is not atheism, because it requires that the sentence 'There are no gods' is meaningless. No more than a couple of decades later, W.V.O. Quine responded with the proposal that we take 'there are gods' to be false if 'god' is meaningless, which gives us that 'there are no gods' is true if 'god' is meaningless (Quine 1960: 229). Here, I have sided with Quine in this dispute.

Some have proposed extension of the fourfold distinction that we have adopted. For example, Rauch (2003), Phipps (2013), and von Hegner (2016) propose that we adopt the term '**apatheist**' to describe those who have no interest in thinking about—never mind arguing about—whether there are gods. Proponents of the term claim that it cross-cuts the fourfold distinction: there are theists, agnostics and atheists who are apatheists, and there are theists, agnostics and atheists who are not apatheists. However, it seems to me that you could not be a theist or an atheist unless you had sufficient interest in the claim that there are gods to form an opinion about it. If that's right, then those who have no interest in thinking about whether there are gods are agnostics: they have given enough attention to the claim to understand it, but not enough attention to form a judgment concerning its truth or falsity. And, if you have formed a judgment concerning the truth or falsity of a controversial claim, and then have no interest in thinking or arguing about it, you are plausibly reckoned a dogmatist. So I am sceptical that we need a new term to describe those who have no interest in thinking about whether there are gods.

2.8 *COMPATIBILITY WITH RELIGION*

Some people think that all atheists are irreligious; some people think that all atheists are anti-religious. In order to assess these claims, we need to understand what it is to be religious (i.e. what it is to belong to a religion).

Following Atran (2002), I take it that what is characteristic of **religion** is that it requires passionate communal displays of costly material commitment to appropriate entities thereby enabling mastery of existential anxieties under ritualised rhythmic sensory coordination in congregation and fellowship. If we suppose that the 'appropriate entities' are gods, then we shall suppose that atheists are, at least, irreligious: they do not believe in the entities that are the focus of passionate communal displays of costly commitments. But gods are not the only 'appropriate entities': there are branches of several major world religions in which, for example, there are passionate communal displays of costly material commitments to means of escaping from cycles of reincarnation and suffering. While many Buddhists believe in gods, and some Buddhists even believe that the Buddha is a god, there are practising Buddhists who do not believe in any gods. Those Buddhists are religious atheists. So, while it is true that many atheists are irreligious—and while it is also true that some atheists are anti-religious—it is also true that some atheists are religious, and neither irreligious nor anti-religious.

While it is not true that all atheists are irreligious, I think that it is true that all materialists, physicalists, naturalists, and humanists are irreligious. The kinds of entities that can serve as the focus of passionate communal displays of costly material commitments that enable mastery of existential anxieties under ritualised rhythmic sensory coordination in congregation and fellowship are non-material, non-physical, non-natural, and non-human. True enough, at least since the establishment of the Cult of Reason during the French Revolution, there have been many attempts to establish 'religions' that have something merely human as the focus of their communal displays. But no 'religion of humanity' has ever succeeded in delivering the goods; no 'religion of humanity' has enabled mastery of existential anxieties about catastrophe, death, deception, disease, injustice, loneliness, loss, pain, want, and the like. Consider, for example, the recent Sunday Assembly movement, which provides for Sunday gatherings in which there is a secular talk, some moments of contemplation, some singing and some socialising (see Addley 2013). While this movement might make some small contribution to the overcoming of loneliness and social isolation, it is incredible to suppose that it will provide significant mastery of anxieties about catastrophe, death, deception, disease, injustice, loss, pain, want, and so on.

Although materialists, physicalists, naturalists and humanists are irreligious, it does not follow that they are anti-religious. Certainly, some materialists, physicalists, naturalists and humanists think that it is deplorable that there are people who engage in passionate communal displays of costly material commitments that enable mastery of existential anxieties under ritualised rhythmic sensory coordination in congregation and fellowship. But other materialists, physicalists, naturalists and humanists maintain that the well-functioning of society depends upon there being passionate communal displays of costly material commitments that enable mastery of existential anxieties under ritualised rhythmic sensory coordination in congregation and fellowship. Historically, this has been *one* significant factor in the widespread reticence of atheists to give public articulation to their beliefs.

2.9 *CONCLUDING REMARKS*

Now that I have set the record straight, let me return to the quotations with which this chapter began.

I do not join with Dawkins in saying that we are all atheists relative to most of the gods that humanity has ever believed in. I would no sooner say that we are all vegans relative to those meals to which we sit down that contain no animal products. Atheists believe that there are no gods. End of story.

I do not join with Jinn in saying that atheism is a religion. There is nothing with respect to which atheism requires passionate communal displays of costly material commitments in aid of mastery of existential anxieties under ritualised rhythmic sensory coordination in congregation and fellowship. Some atheists are religious; others are not. Those atheists who are religious participate in recognised religions such as Buddhism. (I return to this topic in §5.4.)

I do not join with Holbach in saying that children are atheists. On the contrary, sufficiently young children are innocents: they have no conception of gods. Sufficiently young children also have no conception of government, but (despite what long-suffering parents might say) that does not make them little anarchists.

I do not join with Snyder in saying that atheists believe that there are no gods only because, unlike theists, atheists lack the means to perceive gods. Whether there is or can be perception of gods is part of what is in dispute between atheists and theists. Many atheists will respond to Snyder with a similarly loaded barb about seeing what isn't there. I guess atheists could have merely imaginary friends; but why would you?

3

SNAPSHOTS FROM HISTORY

In this chapter, we give very brief accounts of the lives and times of twelve atheists—or reputed atheists—from very different places and very different stages in the history of humanity. Our first four cases—from ancient India, ancient Greece, ancient China, and medieval Syria—are perhaps only 'reputed' atheists: it is very hard to tell whether these people really believed that there are no gods. Our next six cases are two Frenchmen from the eighteenth century, one American from the nineteenth century, and three British citizens from the nineteenth and twentieth centuries. Our last two atheists, from the twenty-first century, are Iranian and Ghanaian, respectively.

3.1 AN ANCIENT INDIAN ATHEIST

Ajita Kesakambali (fl. sixth century BCE) is believed to have been an early Indian materialist. While there is little about him that is known with certainty, it seems that he was a primary source for the teachings of the Cārvāka—Lokāyata, Bṛhaspatya—school of Indian philosophy.

The Cārvāka tradition had largely died out by the end of the twelfth century CE. There is almost nothing written by Cārvāka authors that has survived. Consequently, what is known about the Cārvākas—and, in particular, what is known about Ajita Kesakambali—is based on the writings of authors belonging to competing philosophical traditions. None of those competing traditions is sympathetic to materialism; many of the authors in question are obviously motivated to portray Cārvāka in the least favourable light. For example, according to some sources, Ajita Kesakambali dressed in a blanket of human hair that made him cold when the weather was cold, and hot and foul-smelling when the weather was hot. It is overwhelmingly likely that this is pure propaganda, designed to discredit one of the primary sources of Indian materialism.

Available sources suggest that Ajita Kesakambali taught versions of the following claims: there is no human soul that exists independently of the human body; the human soul is identical to the human body; human beings have an entirely material constitution; there is neither life before birth nor life after death; there is no cycle of reincarnation; death is annihilation; there is neither heaven nor hell; there is no fate; there is no karma; there is no accumulation of karmic merit or demerit that is consequent upon the actions that we perform; good deeds, charity and compassion cannot change the facts about our ultimate annihilation; there are no supernatural causes of natural phenomena; there are no gods; there is no reason to make sacrifices or offerings to the gods, and nothing that is gained if one does so; the scriptures are, by turns, false, tautologous and self-contradictory; there is no scriptural mandate of the authority of particular philosophical schools; there is no divine mandate of the authority of particular philosophical schools; religious rituals merely generate income for priests; rather than give money to priests, people should make donations to the poor; everything of which we can be certain comes to us by way of sense perception. These teachings are all characteristic of the Cārvākas; they are all plausibly attributed to Ajita Kesakambali, on the basis of passages such as the following (from the *Samannaphala Sutta* of the *Digha Nikaya*, cited by Frazier 2013: 370):

> There is nothing bestowed, offered in sacrifice, there is no fruit or result of good or bad deeds, there is not this world or the next ... there are in the world no ascetics or brahmins who have attained, who have perfectly practised, and who proclaim this world and the next, having realised by their own super-knowledge. This human being is composted of the four great elements, and when one dies, the earth reverts to the earth, the fire part to fire, the air part to air, and the faculties pass away into space ... the talk of those who preach a doctrine of survival is vain and false. Fools and wise,

at the breaking up of the body, are destroyed and perish, they do not exist after death.

Available sources suggest that Ajita Kesakambali also taught a version of hedonism: given that there is no authoritative source from which to derive alternative ethical teachings, we should be happy to give some of our time to the pursuit of happiness, or pleasure, or the fulfilment of desires. In the *Sarvasiddhanta Samgraha* (verses 9–12), the following Cārvāka view is elaborated:

> The enjoyment of heaven lies in eating delicious food, ... using fine clothes, perfumes, garlands, sandal paste ... while moksha is death which is cessation of life-breath ... the wise therefore ought not to take pains on account of moksha. A fool wears himself out by penances and fasts. Chastity and other such ordinances are laid down by clever weaklings.

The primary import of these passages, and others of their ilk, is *anti-ascetic*: it is silly not to embrace the pleasures of life, even though these pleasures are sometimes mixed with pains. Despite the representations of these views by their critics—who say that the Cārvākas had no morals or ethics, and that they recommended feasting even at the cost of running oneself into debt—it goes way beyond the evidence to accept that the Cārvākas recommended self-centred pursuit of one's own pleasure and selfish satisfaction of one's own desires. Frazier (2013: 372) notes that, in the *Ain i Akbari*, in an account of a symposium of religions held by the Indian Muslim Emperor Akbar in 1578, the Cārvākas are said to be a 'peasant' movement that defends a kind of common-sense consequentialism (i.e. an ethic that attaches primary importance to the anticipated consequences of actions). Given the paucity of sources, we simply do not know what Ajita Kesakambali's ethics demanded of us in our treatment of one another; however, it is a very plausible conjecture that much of what is handed down to us is libel based on conflation of anti-asceticism with ethical egoism.

There is a fuller record of atheistic traditions in Indian philosophy than there is in Greek and Roman philosophy. It is not clear why this is the case. According to some, the Cārvākas were also called 'Lokāyata' because the espoused 'the worldview of the people'. It is hard to believe that among the Greeks and Romans who belonged to the lower social classes—i.e. among those who were not nobles, or priests, or merchants, or soldiers, or function-aries of government, or the like—there were none who came to the kinds of beliefs that Ajita Kesakambali maintained. However, while the Cārvākas are written into the history of Indian thought—if only as renegades whose views are to be vanquished—there seems to be no such recording of 'the views of the people' in the history of Greek and Roman thought.

3.2 *AN ANCIENT GREEK ATHEIST*

Diagoras of Melos (fl. fifth century BCE) was known through-out the ancient world as Diagoras 'the Atheist'. Nonetheless, it is at best uncertain whether he was an atheist. While some (e.g. Whitmarsh 2015)—argue that atheism flourished more in ancient Greece and pre-Christian Rome than in most subsequent civilisations, it is not easy to find *any* clear examples of classical Greek and Roman atheists. Certainly, there were many, follow-ing the early lead of Xenophanes of Colophon (*c.*570–*c.*475 BCE), who ridiculed traditional religious views. And there were undisputed agnostics, such as Protagoras (*c.*490–*c.*421)—said to have been charged with impiety, killed or exiled, and subject to a burning of all of books, including his treatise *On The Gods*, by the Athenians—and sceptics such as Sextus Empiricus (*c.*160–*c.*210 CE). But even the ancient atomists—such as Democritus (*c.*460–*c.*370 BCE)—and other early materialists—such as Epicurus (341–270 BCE)—believed that there is at least one god. The same seems also to have been true for Prodicus (465–395 BCE), who regarded the popular gods as personifications of things that contribute to the comfort of our lives: the sun, the moon, rivers, fountains, forests, fields, and so forth.

Diagoras was a minor poet. The content of the fragments of his poetry that survive does not justify attribution of atheism to him; indeed, according to Woodbury (1965: 179), they testify to a conventional piety in religion. Later sources say various things about him that have proven very difficult to substantiate: that he profaned the Eleusinian Mysteries and revealed its secrets; that he was tried by the Athenian Assembly; that he fled Athens; that the

Athenians set a reward for his killing or capture; that he was the author of two atheistic treatises that circulated in the centuries after his death; that, as reported by Cicero, he responded to a friend's attempt to convince him of the existence of gods—by pointing to votive pictures telling how 'vows to the gods' had saved people from storms at sea—with the observation that 'there are nowhere any pictures of those who have been wrecked or drowned at sea'; that he chopped up a wooden statue of Hercules so that the god could undertake a thirteenth labour of boiling his turnips (or, perhaps, lentils); that he was the lover of Nicodorus of Mantinea, and his associate in legislation; that he was both the slave and the student of Democritus; that he was the centre of a school of physicists; that he converted to atheism as the result of an experience—possibly successful plagiarism and perjury by a fellow poet, or maybe the embezzlement of a trust—that caused him to doubt the justice of the gods; that he was found in possession of an atheistic book at the time of his death; and that his radical atheism was due to his seduction by 'the false wisdom of the east'.

Woodbury (1965: 210f.) speculates that, like the poet Cinesias, Diagoras may have been a member of a roistering club devoted to flouting the rules and observances of popular piety. If so, then given his Melian ancestry, and given that Melos fell to the Athenians in 416 BCE—with accompanying slaughter of all Melian men and enslavement of all Melian women and children—it is understandable why, in Athens in 415 BCE, Diagoras was targeted by the Athenian Assembly for his alleged profanation of the Eleusinian Mysteries (i.e. of the annual initiations of the cult of Demeter and Persephone, the acme of the secret religious rites of ancient Greece). However, it is mere speculation that Diagoras belonged to a club of this kind. Indeed, there is not much about Diagoras that is anything other than conjectural. The most recent comprehensive assessment of Diagoras—by Winiarczyk (2016)—concludes that there is very little that we can assert with confidence, although, on the balance of the evidence, we should be fairly sceptical that he was an atheist.

Theodorus of Cyrene (*c*.340–*c*.250 BCE) is another ancient philosopher who was called 'The Atheist'. Diogenes Laertius says that Theodorus was alleged to have told Euryclides the hierophant that the priest himself was guilty of profaning the Mysteries because he explained them to initiates during the course of their initiation; that he was sceptical about all judgments about gods; that he asserted that nothing is wrong *per se*; that he claimed that a wise man should not risk his own life for his country to help the fools for whom all moral principles have been created; and that the whole world is his home (rather than any particular city within it). While there are historical sources which report that Theodorus was tried and executed by the Athenian Assembly, Filonik (2013: 76) suggests that the most that might plausibly be supposed is that Theodorus left Athens in fear of charges of impiety. As in the case of Diagoras of Melos, the stories that have grown up around Theodorus of Cyrene have diverse political and religious motivations. At our historical distance, it is more or less impossible to sift the wheat from the chaff. Nonetheless, on the balance of the evidence, it seems that we have good reason to be sceptical that Theodorus of Cyrene really was an atheist.

While we have been at some pains to argue that Diagoras of Melos and Theodorus of Cyrene were not atheists (i.e. not among those who believe that there are no gods), we can explain why they were given the label 'atheist'. As Bremmer (2007: 22) notes, all parties in Mediterranean antiquity—Greeks, Romans, pagans, and Christians—quickly developed an appreciation of the utility of the pejorative 'atheist' as a label for those who deny the existence of the gods in which those who are applying the label—or even, in some cases, others—believe. Whether or not Diagoras of Melos and Theodorus of Cyrene actually denied the existence of the popular Athenian gods, the belief that they denied the existence of the popular Athenian gods suffices to explain—and even, in a certain sense, to justify—the application of the label 'atheist' to them.

3.3 *AN ANCIENT CHINESE ATHEIST*

Wang Chong (27–*c*.100 CE) was born into a poor Chinese family at a time when Daoism and Confucianism had both become deeply superstitious: Confucius and Laozi were widely taken to be gods, there was almost universal belief in ghosts, divinatory practices were ubiquitous, and the practice of feng shui was rampant. Reacting against this state of affairs, Wang Chong developed a view of the universe and the place of human beings within it that insisted upon reason, experience, and replicable experiment. While it is not clear that it is right to say—as some commentators do—that his views are naturalistic and mechanistic, it is true that he developed a vast array of original objections to the superstitious beliefs of his contemporaries. Moreover, he tried—albeit with mixed success—to develop empirically supported explanations of natural phenomena: while, unlike his Chinese contemporaries, he had the water cycle more or less correct, also, unlike his Chinese contemporaries, he had a completely erroneous explanation of eclipses and the shining of the moon.

Despite his lowly circumstances, Wang Chong studied at the Imperial University in Luoyang. Legend has it that, because he could not afford to buy textbooks, he relied on his prodigious memory in the course of lengthy periods of reading in book-shops to carry out his education; legend also has it that he developed a deep antipathy for those who were admired merely for their position, power, and wealth. He had brief periods of employment—in teaching and the public service—and was about to take up an appointment as a senior scholar in the court of the Emperor at the time of his death. His reputation rested on his essays—on diverse subjects, including philosophy, mor-ality, government, criticism, and macrobiotics—eighty-five of which were collected together in his major work, the *Lun-heng*. While his work had little impact during his own lifetime, it did play a significant role in the subsequent development of a 'new' Daoism that was stripped of the superstitious and mystical ele-ments to which he objected.

Here is Wang Chong on 'the purposeless heavens':

> By the fusion of the matter and energy of the heavens and earth, all things of the world are produced spontaneously—just as by the mix-ture of matter and energy of husband and wife children are born spontaneously. Among the things thus produced, creatures with blood in their veins are sensitive of hunger and cold. Seeing that the five grains can be eaten, they use them as food; and discovering that silk and hemp can be worn, they take them and wear them. Some people are of the opinion that the heavens produce grain for the purpose of feeding mankind, and silk and hemp to clothe them. That

would be tantamount to making the heavens the farmer of man, or his mulberry girl; it would not be in accordance with spontaneity, therefore this opinion is very questionable and unacceptable.

(Wang 1907: 4)

And here is Wang Chong on 'the indifferent heavens':

If the heavens had produced creatures on purpose, they ought to have taught them to love each other, and not prey upon and destroy one another. One might object that such is the nature of the five elements, that when the heavens create all things, they are imbued with the matter and energies of the five elements, and that these fight together and destroy one another. But then the heavens ought to have filled creatures with the matter and energy of one element alone, and taught them mutual love, not permitting the forces of the five elements to resort to strife and mutual destruction.

(Wang 1907: 5)

On Wang Chong's view, heaven is merely a realm of atmospheric and astronomical objects and events that belong to the same physical domain as the earth; it is not an entity that is imbued with intentionality, and it is not subject to normative guidance. In the passages above, we see Wang Chong making arguments directed at his Daoist contemporaries who do suppose that heaven is capable of intentional action and that heaven can answer to normative demands. The text on indifferent heavens has obvious affinities with the arguments of Western free-thinkers who claim that an omnipotent, perfectly good God ought to have made a better world than the one in which we find ourselves.

It is not clear whether Wang Chong is an atheist; it is not clear whether he wants to abolish Confucianism and Daoism, or whether he merely wants to reform them. What is clear is that he was a brave and original thinker who was quite out of step with the times in which he lived. Many of his own arguments seem weak and strange to us. Consider, for example:

There is a belief that, by the doctrine of Laozi, one can continue into another existence. Through quietism and extirpation of desire one nourishes the vital force and cherishes the spirit. ... But what are the passions of plants and shrubs, that cause them to die in the autumn after being born in the spring? They are dispassionate, yet their lives do not extend further than one year. Men are full of passions and desires, yet they can become one hundred years old. Thus the dispassionate die prematurely and the passionate live long. Hence Laozi's account of how to extend life into another mode of existence by means of quietism and extirpation of desire is wrong.

(Wang 1907: 26)

Nonetheless, even though he did not always find the best objections to make to those with whom he disagreed, his opinions have a remarkably greater consonance with our opinions than do the opinions of his Confucian and Daoist contemporaries. While it probably goes beyond the available evidence to claim Wang Chong as an atheist—or as a materialist, or as a naturalist, or as a rationalist, or as a secular humanist—he is clearly someone who had no time for the foolishness of traditional religion and who was not prepared to spare those who deserved to be met with thoughtful criticism.

3.4 A MEDIEVAL SYRIAN ATHEIST

Abu al-ʿAla' al-Maʿarri (973–1057 CE) was born in the Syrian town of Maʿarra at the scientific and cultural peak of what is often referred to as 'the Islamic Golden Age'. Despite being blinded by smallpox soon after his fourth birthday, al-Maʿarri was one of the great classical poets and a fiercely independent freethinker who produced scathing condemnations of theistic religion. While al-Maʿarri pursued his education in various Syrian towns, including Aleppo and Antioch, and while he spent some time in literary salons in Baghdad, he lived out the last fifty years of his life in seclusion in Maʿarra, practising an ascetic lifestyle and following a vegan diet. Al-Maʿarri was noted for his negative views on life, as well as for his opposition to dogmatism and superstition, and his insistence on the superiority of the deliverances of reason to the claims of authority and tradition. Al-Maʿarri's major works include: *The Tinder Spark* (Saqṭ al-zand), *Unnecessary Necessity* (Luzūm mā lam yalzam), *The Epistle of Forgiveness* (Risālat al-ghufrān) and *Paragraphs* *and Periods* (Al-Fuṣūl wa al-ghāyāt). The *Tinder Spark* and *Unnecessary Necessity* are collections of poems; *Paragraphs and Periods* is a collection of homilies, perhaps intended as a parody of the Qu'ran. *The Epistle of Forgiveness*—al-Maʿarri's best known work—is a prose poem that is often compared to Dante's *Divine Comedy*; the first complete English translation of *The Epistle of Forgiveness* appeared as al-Ma'arri (2016).

Owing to the difficulties involved in the translation of poetry, renderings of al-Maʿarri's texts vary widely. For example, here as two different translations of the same well-known passage:

> They all err—Muslims, Jews,
> Christians and Zoroastrians
> Humanity follows two world-wide sects
> One, man intelligent without religion
> The second, religious without intellect
> (Nicholson (1921)

> Hanifs are stumbling, Christians all astray
> Jews wildered, Magians far on error's way
> We mortals are composed of two great schools
> Enlightened knaves or else religious fools
> (Nicholson 1907)

Elsewhere, the last part of this is rendered: 'The inhabitants of the earth are of two sorts: those with brains but no religion, and those with religion but no brains' (Malik 2011). Whichever reading we follow, it is clear that al-Maʿarri is a caustic critic of all of the religions with which he is familiar. Moreover, his worldview is deeply pessimistic. Consider:

> Better for Adam and all who issued from his loins
> That he and they, yet unborn, created never had been!
> For whilst his body was dust and rotten bones in the earth
> Ah, did he feel what his children saw and suffered of woe.
> (Nicholson 1921)

And:

> We laugh, but inept is our laughter;
> We should weep and weep sore,
> Who are shattered like glass, and thereafter
> Remoulded no more.
>
> (Nicholson 1921)

Some (e.g. Yeghiyan 1945: 232f.) propose to explain al-Ma'arri's dark anger as the outcome of the disfigurement and disability that was caused by his childhood illness. But it is not clear that this takes adequate account of the rationalism that was bequeathed to him by the *falsafah* tradition in Islamic philosophy, initiated by Al-Farabi (*c.* 872–951), and advanced, during the lifetime of al-Ma'arri, by ibn Sina (980–1037). While most of the *falsafah* were conventional Muslims who took the Qu'ran to be the word of God, they thought that the truths of the Qu'ran could be arrived at by the use of human reason, without the support of revelation and tradition. Moreover, they supposed that we have a philosophical duty to live according to the dictates of reason, in accordance with the divine law that governs our universe. Although the views of the *falsafah* were consistent with traditional Islamic piety, they opened the door to an independent rationalism which rejected all religion, and took reason to be the sole guide to truth:

> Traditions come from the past, of high import if they be true;
> Aye, but weak is the chain of those who warrant their truth.
> Consult thy reason and let perdition take other all:
> Of all the conference Reason best will counsel and guide.
>
> (Nicholson 1921)

Al-Ma'arri is one of the great *zindiqs*—freethinking heretics—of the Islamic Golden Age, a status that was only made possible by the *falsafah* tradition in Islamic philosophy. Even so, one might wonder how al-Ma'arri was able to speak and publish as he did, given the challenges that he presented to Islamic orthodoxy, and given that he was the subject of accusations of heresy throughout his life.

They recite their sacred books, although the fact informs me
That these are a fiction from first to last.
O Reason, thou (alone) speakest the truth.
Then perish the fools who forged the religious traditions or inter-
preted them.

(Nicholson (1921).)

Part of the reason, no doubt, is that, as al-Maʿarri himself recommended to others, he included many orthodox passages in his poetry, to which he could point if accusations of heresy arose. But it is seems doubtful that that is the full story. Perhaps—though this is merely speculation—al-Maʿarri was so admired for his poetic skills, his honesty, his integrity, and his unflinching intelligence that he was tolerated by those not naturally disposed to tolerance.

For his own epitaph, al-Maʿarri, who chose not to marry and to remain childless, wrote:

This wrong was by my father done
To me, but never by me to one

In the 1940s, in preparation for the millennial celebration of his birth, al-Ma'arri's tomb was rebuilt; in 2013, a statue of al-Maʿarri in Maʿarra was beheaded by members of the al-Nusra Front. Even now, he remains a controversial figure in the Islamic world.

Whether al-Maʿarri was an atheist is not entirely clear. As we have already noted, there are passages in his poetry that suggest conventional theistic belief. But, as we have also noted, he himself tells us that it is sometimes prudent to dissimulate. While there is nothing that definitively rules out his possession of deistic beliefs, there is also nothing that clearly establishes that he is a theist. Let me leave him with the last word:

So, too, the creeds of man: the one prevails
Until the other comes; and this one fails
When that one triumphs; aye, the lonesome world
Will always want the latest fairy tales.

(Nicholson 1921)

3.5 *AN EIGHTEENTH-CENTURY FRENCH ATHEIST*

Jean Meslier (1664–1729) appeared to be a largely unremarkable Catholic priest in the small village of Etrépigny in the Ardennes. However, during his final decade, he wrote a *Testament* that revealed that he had been leading a double life. For, while he was performing the duties of a rural priest—to the point of distributing the annual balance of his income to his poorer parishioners—he was also compiling the thoughts of an atheist, materialist, hedonist, anarchist, internationalist, revolutionary philosopher. Following his death, copies of his *Testament* circulated in Paris. In 1761, Voltaire published his *Extract of the Sentiments of Jean Meslier*, which pre-served Meslier's criticisms of religion, miracles, prophecies, and Christian dogma, but omitted Meslier's defences of atheism, materialism, hedonism, and radical politics. In 1772, Holbach published an abridged version of his own *System of Nature* under the title *The Good Sense of Curé Meslier* (a nod to the influence that Meslier's *Testament* had on Holbach and his coterie). In 1790, Sylvain Maréchal published *The Catechism of Curé Meslier*, which was an attempt to summarise the highlights of Meslier's *Testament*. And, in 1795, the Marquis de Sade published *Philosophy in the Boudoir*, a work whose philosophical parts were deeply influenced by Meslier's *Testament*. The first publication of the full text of Meslier's *Testament* did not appear until 1864; the first English translation appeared in 2009.

Meslier's *Testament* is a sprawling, formless, repetitive work that, at his death, had run to more than 1000 pages. Onfray (2006) claims that Meslier 'proposes the first atheist thinking in Western history'. While that claim seems unlikely to be true—consider, for example, that Kazimierz Łyszczyński (1634–1689) had his tongue pulled out and was then beheaded for his authorship of a treatise entitled *The Non-Existence of God*—it is clear that Meslier is an atheist who maintains that we have overwhelming evidence against the existence of the Christian God and who develops a materialist metaphysics that leaves no place for any other gods.

Meslier's critique of Christianity has many dimensions. The Christian God is said to be good, kind, loving, just, and merciful, and yet: gets depicted in scripture as jealous, angry, vindictive, aggressive, wicked, demanding, unjust, capricious, dreadful, cruel and obsessively demanding of our obedience; sends unbaptised children to limbo, parks most of us in purgatory, and sentences many of us to eternal damnation for unimportant 'sins'; permits misery, poverty, wickedness, evil, exploitation, social injustice and the connivances of the Catholic Church; deliberately chooses not to create a world in which there is nothing but good; hides and sets up barriers to invocation, prayer, and intercession; and becomes angered by violations of arbitrary commandments. The Christian Bible is said to be the word of the Christian God, and yet it is: full of contradictions, absurdities and lies; unreliable, patched together to serve political interests, and primarily intended to consolidate the temporal power of the Church; obviously properly classified with folklore and fiction; and not properly defended as allegorical, since that line licences every kind of interpretative fantasy. The miracles of the Christian prophets, just like the miracles of the pagans, contradict everything we know about how the world works, as do all of the other Biblical myths; even if there were such events, they could not possibly be squared with divine benevolence, rationality, consistency and justice, and would instead be evidence of divine malice and cruelty. Contrary to the apotheosis of Christ, the scriptural evidence suggests that Jesus was a despicable fanatic, lunatic, rogue, liar, and false prophet whose words and deeds are very unreliably recorded in the gospels, which disagree on so many points of detail. The Catholic Church is vile, pernicious, and wedded to absurd dogma (e.g. the Trinity) and tradition (e.g. the Eucharist) that are plainly in conflict with an honest materialism. Finally, Christian morality loves and cherishes misery and suffering on the absurd grounds that this reflects the Passion of Christ: it condemns desires even though these are natural affections that conduce to the future existence of humanity; it absurdly commends continence and chastity when consenting adults should be free to engage in mutually chosen acts even beyond the bounds of marriage; it causes great suffering for many women and children because it forbids divorce; it causes great suffering for animals because it teaches that we can do to them whatever we choose; it absurdly commands turning the other cheek in the face of feudal brutality and exploitation of the weak and vulnerable; it is complicit in the excesses of tyrants, parasitic nobles, and their priestly enablers; and it is a counter-revolutionary force that endorses the status quo and gives generic blessing to the reigning of injustice upon the lower classes by the upper classes.

Meslier's alternative to the Christian worldview is based upon a rather inchoate materialism that recognises space, time, and matter as the fundamental ingredients of causal reality. According to Meslier, the primary cause of human suffering is that, given feudal modes of social organisation, there are too many people competing for too few resources, a condition that might be ameliorated under a different distribution of wealth and property. Meslier supposes that all people have rights to life—food, clothing, housing, healthcare, education—liberty, gainful employment and freedom. Further, he supposes that, under feudal modes of social organisation, there is a class struggle between, on the one hand, peasants and workers, and, on the other hand, kings, nobles, judges, lawyers, priests and the Church, with the desire of the latter to see the former grovel being a primary determinant of class hatred. His favoured solution is revolution. The lower classes should simply: stop paying taxes; refuse feudal rent; rebel against forced labour; abolish private property; and kill the enemies of humanity. Moreover, he thinks that this solution should be global: everywhere on the planet, the lower classes should join a struggle that will end only when 'the last of the nobles is strangled with the intestines of the last priest'. Finally—echoing other sentiments that subsequently emerged during the Enlightenment—Meslier notes that, while intellectuals are not on the side of the peasants and the workers, and are conspicuously absent from the companionship of the wretched of the earth, the future for intellectuals is to join the class struggle on the side of the lower classes.

3.6 ANOTHER EIGHTEENTH-CENTURY FRENCH ATHEIST

Paul-Henri d'Holbach (1723–1789) ran the most influential *salon* in Paris between the 1750s and the 1780s. His dinner parties were attended by ambassadors and nobles from across Europe, as well as by the most famous intellectuals—actors, chemists, economists, historians, mathematicians, novelists, philosophers, social critics, etc.—of the age, including Jean d'Alembert, Cesare Beccaria, Etienne Condillac, Marie Condorcet, Benjamin Franklin,

David Garrick, Edward Gibbon, Claude-Adrien Helvétius, David Hume, Joseph Priestley, Jean-Jacques Rousseau, Adam Smith, Thomas Sterne, and Horace Walpole. There was also a privileged coterie of about a dozen who were regular attendees, including Denis Diderot and Jacques-Andre Naigeon. The members of the coterie were political radicals with revolutionary agendas; many— including Holbach himself—were avowed atheists.

Holbach was raised by an uncle who had made a fortune on the stock exchange, and who threw fabulous parties. When Holbach was about thirty years old, his uncle died, and Holbach inherited a considerable fortune, much of which he used to continue his uncle's legacy. As Lebuffe (2014) notes, it is remarkable that Holbach was able to maintain a *salon* in which political and religious reformers met freely with visitors who were unaccustomed to open dialogue, and, in many cases, part of the establishment that the coterie wished to bring down. Lebuffe suggests a tripartite explanation: Holbach was a remarkably fine character; his generosity at table was unstinting (the food and wine were genuinely superb); and he was not seen to be as radical as the other members of his coterie. However, even if Holbach was not taken to be so radical, his books—which he published anonymously—were notorious; but his authorship of these books did not become common knowledge until the early part of the nineteenth century, many years after his death.

Holbach was a voluminous writer. He contributed, either by writing or translating, four hundred entries to Diderot's *Encyclopédie*—a work which, according to Diderot, was intended to change the way that people thought, and which played a significant role in the lead up to the French Revolution—on topics ranging over politics, religion, chemistry and mineralogy. His best-known works, among more than fifty books that he authored or co-authored, include *Christianity Unveiled* (1766), *Letters for Eugenia* (1768), *Ecce Homo! A Critical History of Jesus Christ* (1769), *The System Of Nature* (1770), *Good Sense* (1772), *Natural Politics* (1773), *The Social System* (1773), *Universal Morality* (1776), and *Ethocracy* (1776). Holbach defends a mechanistic metaphysics which maintains that nature consists of nothing but matter in motion under mechanical laws, and a naturalistic ethics and politics which claims that human behaviour is properly understood in terms of psychological and social laws. In Holbach's view, ethics is enlightened self-interest: since virtue can only be inculcated in people who seek to pursue their own interests in their natural surroundings, religion is entirely a source of unhappiness and vice. Moreover, in Holbach's view, the primary purpose of politics is the securing of general welfare: where governments fail to secure property, freedom of speech and freedom of religion, people have the right to revolt, and to insist that the government does what it is supposed to do.

While there are aspects of Holbach's thought that are genuinely novel—for example, as Lebuffe (2016) explains, Holbach recast Locke's distinction between primary and secondary qualities as a distinction between properties that all material bodies possess and properties that only some material bodies possess—his defence of atheism follows well-worn and predictable paths. In particular, Holbach emphasises: the difficulties involved in the intelligible discussion of something that is intrinsically unknowable; the unsatisfactory nature of descriptions of God that use only negations of genuinely descriptive terms (e.g. 'infinite' = 'not finite', 'impassable' = 'not affected by other things', and so forth); the highly suspect psychological origins of theistic belief (e.g. in fear of death); and the difficulties that arise when one tries to reconcile the alleged perfection of God with the horrific evils that abound in our universe. Nonetheless, at the time that Holbach was rehearsing these considerations, he risked public condemnation—and perhaps much worse—if his authorship of his anonymous books became public knowledge.

In the *Appendix* to *The System of Nature*, chapters XXVI–XXVIII, Holbach writes as follows:

> Men tremble at the very name of an atheist. But who is an atheist? The man who brings mankind back to reason and experience, by destroying prejudices inimical to their happiness; who has no need of resorting to supernatural powers in explaining the phenomena of nature. ... It is true, the number of atheists is inconsiderable, because enthusiasm has dazzled the human mind, and the progress of error has been so very great, that few men have courage to search for truth. ... An atheist does not believe in the existence of God. No man can be certain of the existence of an inconceivable being,

in whom inconsistent attributes are said to be united. ... No sensible atheist thinks that the cruel actions caused by religion are capable of being justified. If the atheist be a bad man, he knows when he is committing wrong. Neither God nor his priests can then persuade him that he has been acting properly. ... We cannot expect to take away from a whole nation its religious ideas, because they have been inculcated from the tenderest infancy. But the vulgar, in the long run, may reap advantages from labours, of which they at present have no idea. Atheism, having truth on its side, will gradually insinuate itself into the mind, and become familiar to man.

Whereas Jean Meslier was unable to share his atheistic ideas directly with anyone else, Paul-Henri d'Holbach belonged to a circle of like-minded atheists who shared his vision of converting the whole world to atheism. With the assistance of Diderot, who may have shared the writing of some of the works that we now attribute to Holbach, Naigeon, who was Holbach's literary executor, and the other members of his coterie, Holbach was able—albeit anonymously—to make a start on the project of arguing with theists about the existence of God, the harms and benefits of religion, and so on.

3.7 *A NINETEENTH-CENTURY BRITISH ATHEIST*

Mary Ann Evans (1819–1880) was the daughter of the manager of the Arbury Hall Estate in Warwickshire. After her formal education ended when she was sixteen, she was given access to the library at Arbury Hall. With some assistance from tutors, she became fluent in Greek, Latin, French, German and Italian—and, later in life, Hebrew and Spanish—with a broad knowledge of classical and current thought and literature; she was also an accomplished pianist.

When her formal education ended, Evans was a devout Christian. After she and her father moved to Foleshill, near Coventry, she joined the progressive, freethinking circle of Charles Bray, a wealthy ribbon manufacturer: contact with people such as Robert Owen, Herbert Spencer, Harriet Martineau and Ralph Waldo Emerson exacerbated the developing religious doubts that had been seeded by her independent reading. One longer-term outcome of her introduction to liberal theology and freethought was her translation of Strauss's *The Life of Jesus* (1846), Feuerbach's *The Essence of Christianity* (1854), and—though it remained unpublished at the time of her death—Spinoza's *Ethics* (1856).

In the early 1850s, Evans was employed by John Chapman as assistant editor of the *Westminster Review*, to which she, herself, regularly contributed essays and reviews, and of which, in practice, she was chief editor. During this time, she began living with George Henry Lewes—a noted scientists, philosopher, actor, and critic—who, for complex reasons, was unable to obtain a divorce from his estranged wife. With Lewes's encouragement, Evans turned her attention to writing novels and, under the name 'George Eliot', produced *Adam Bede* (1859), *The Mill on the Floss* (1860), *Silas Marner* (1861), *Romola* (1863), *Felix Holt: The Radical* (1866), *Middlemarch* (1872), and *Daniel Deronda* (1876), along with numerous volumes of poetry and criticism.

Following Lewes's death in 1878, Evans spent two years pre-paring Lewes's three-volume *Problems of Life and Mind* for publica-tion. In mid-1880, she married a much younger man, John Cross. However, the combination of a throat infection and kidney disease carried her off about seven months after their wedding. The rela-tionship between Evans and Lewes was considered scandalous—officially, 'adulterous'—and this, together with her well-known atheism, ruled out burial in Westminster Abbey. Instead, she is buried with Lewes at Highgate Cemetery, in a corner reserved for atheists and agnostics. However, that's not to say that Evans and Lewes were not readmitted to 'polite society' during their life together. Despite the 'shocking' nature of her private life, Evans's novels were enormously popular: Queen Victoria was a fan, so taken with *Adam Bede* that she commissioned Edward Corbould to paint scenes from it.

Although Evans was an atheist—she believed that there are no gods and that there is no life after death—she remained sympa-thetic both to religion and, in particular, to Christianity. Her view, developed in the course of her reading of Feuerbach, was that religion gives appropriate expression to important human needs and desires and that Christianity is the highest form of religion. Thus, while she supposed that the doctrines of Christianity are false, and that there is no historical truth in the Bible, she also supposed that Christianity provided the best available 'projection' of our 'inner humanity'. Despite her dismissal of dogmatic theology, Evans believed in both duties to others and subordination of the self. Moreover, she sympathised with what she took to the driving motive for religious belief: our need to manage the existential anxieties that arise for us in the course of our lives in a vast and indifferent universe that deals us catastrophe, deception, disease, injustice, loneliness, loss, pain, want, and, ultimately, death. On her view, as things stand, it would be wrong to deny people the consolations of Christianity.

Evans's views about religion and Christianity were not to the taste of all other atheists. For example, in *Twilight of the Idols*, Nietzsche (1888/1976: 515) wrote:

> G. Eliot.—They are rid of the Christian God and now believe all the more firmly that they must abide by Christian morality. That is an English consistency: we do not wish to hold it against little moralistic females à la Eliot. In England, one must rehabilitate oneself after every little emancipation from theology by showing in a veritably awe-inspiring manner what a moral fanatic one is. There is the penance they pay there.

I am tempted to see Nietzsche as an outlier here. True enough, many of those who followed in the footsteps of Meslier were keen to see the back of Christianity. However, as the example of Holbach suggests, most of them supposed that it had to be replaced with something else. In particular, many atheists were keen to think through alternative social and political arrangements that would ameliorate the conditions under which most of us live. Many supposed that there would need to be civic cults (e.g. cults of reason) that replaced religious rituals and festivals. More importantly, many also supposed that a secular morality that had substantial overlap with Christian morality would be required under any workable social and political arrangements. Society is founded upon human relationships that cannot function in the absence of at least some subordination of self and recognition of duties towards others. It may be true that Christian morality valorises subordination of self and recognition of duties to others, but there is nothing essentially Christian in either of these things. Whatever you think about Evans's positive estimation of Christianity, it just seems wrong to criticise it on account of Christianity's commitment to moral teachings—concerning subordination of the self and recognition of duties to others—that are properly taken to be universal.

Even if you accept this response to Nietzsche's criticism of Evans, you might be tempted to think that Evans's view is insufficiently radical. Once we've recognised that the doctrines of Christianity are false, surely we should be looking new forms of social organisation that can make an honest accommodation with that recognition. Even if Christianity is the highest form of religion, why think that we cannot replace it with a better secular substitute? Be all of this as it may, no one can accuse our *next* featured atheist of being insufficiently radical.

3.8 A NINETEENTH-CENTURY AMERICAN ATHEIST

Emma Goldman (1869–1940) was a self-identified anarchist. Born in Korno, Lithuania—in the then Russian Empire—Goldman migrated to the United States in 1885. Following the trial, conviction and execution of a group of anarchists who were allegedly responsible for a bombing in Haymarket Square in Chicago in 1886, Goldman became an activist, lecturing to large crowds on property, government, militarism, freedom of speech, atheism, women's rights, gay rights, and violence. In 1892, with Alexander Berkman—her lifelong friend and lover—Goldman planned the assassination of Henry Clay Frick, an industrialist and financier employed by Andrew Carnegie during the Homestead strike; when the assassination attempt failed, Berkman was sentenced to 22 years' imprisonment. In 1893, when the United States was in severe economic trouble and unemployment was running at over 20 per cent, Goldman was arrested for incitement to riot during a speech to nearly 3000 people in Union Square, New York, and sentenced to a year's imprisonment on Blackwell Island. In the mid-1890s, Goldman studied midwifery and massage in Vienna, and met various famous anarchists, including Peter Kropotkin, Errico Malatesta, and Louise Michel; thereafter, in the United States, she was able to make cross-country tours, giving lectures and supporting herself with midwifery. In 1901, Goldman was arrested and detained for two weeks after Leon Czolgosz assassinated William McKinley because Czolgosz claimed to have been motivated to act by one of Goldman's lectures; to the dismay of her fellow anarchists, including Berkman, Goldman refused to condemn Czolgosz's action, even after his execution. In 1906, Goldman launched *Mother Earth*, a journal for anarchists and other radical activists; in 1914, she joined forces with Margaret Sanger to advocate 'birth control' and was arrested for giving public lessons on the use of contraceptives. In 1917, Goldman and Berkman were arrested for their organisation of the No Conscription League in New York; upon their release from prison, they were deported to Russia under the Anarchist Exclusion Act. Although they were initially enthusiastic about the Russian Revolution, they found the Soviet state repressive; by 1921, they had relocated to Berlin, where Goldman wrote *My Disillusionment in Russia* (1923) and *My Further Disillusionment in Russia* (1924). In 1925, Goldman and Berkman reached London, where Goldman acquired British citizenship by 'marrying' the Scottish anarchist James Colton. Between 1928 and 1930, Goldman lived in Saint-Tropez, writing her best-selling autobiography, *Living My Life*. During the Spanish Civil War, Goldman was an enthusiastic correspondent for the CNT-FAI, until they started cooperating with Communist forces in order to mount joint resistance to Franco's fascists. After her death in 1940, Goldman was buried in Forest Park, Chicago, in near proximity to other anarchists and social activists, including those executed after the Haymarket Square bombing. Since the early 1970s, Goldman has been the subject of numerous plays, novels, films, dissertations, and other scholarly works; her extraordinary life is nicely encapsulated in the apocryphal attribution: 'If I can't dance, I don't want to be in your revolution.'

In 1908, Goldman wrote a small, personal manifesto, with the title 'What I Believe', that was published in the *New York World*. This paper serves as a fine introduction to her (then) thoughts on a wide range of topics (Goldman 1908):

> 'Property' means dominion over things and the denial to others of the use of those things. ... Productivity of labour within the last few decades has increased so tremendously ... (as) to make property not only a hindrance to human well-being, but ... a deadly barrier to all progress.

> Government ... is necessary only to maintain or protect property and monopoly. ... As a promoter of individual liberty, human well-being and social harmony ... government stands condemned. ... Anarchism—the absence of government—will ensure the widest and greatest scope for unhampered human development.
>
> The military spirit is the most merciless, heartless, and brutal in existence. ... A standing army and navy ... is indicative of the decay of liberty and of the destruction of all this best and finest in our nation. Many good people imagine that the principles of free speech or press can be exercised properly and safely within the limits of constitutional guarantees. That is the only excuse ... for the terrible apathy and indifference to the onslaught upon free speech and press that we have witnessed in this country.
>
> Religion is a superstition that originated in man's inability to understand natural phenomena. The Church is an organised institution that has always been a stumbling block to progress.
>
> Marriage is often a purely economic arrangement, furnishing the woman with a life-long life insurance policy, and the man with a perpetuator of his kind or a pretty toy. Marriage ... prepares the woman for the life of a parasite, a dependent, helpless servant, while it furnishes the man the right of a chattel mortgage over a human life.
>
> Anarchism is the only philosophy of peace, the only theory of the social relationship that values human life above everything else. ... Some anarchists have committed acts of violence, but it is terrible economic inequality and great political injustice that prompts such acts, not anarchism.

In addition to the topics mentioned in this manifesto, Goldman was also a passionate defender of gay rights, at a time when no one else publicly defended those rights. In Goldman (1923) she writes:

> It is a tragedy, I feel, that people of a different sexual type are caught in a world which shows so little understanding for homosexuals and is so crassly indifferent to the various gradations and variations of gender and their great significance in life.

As these excerpts make clear, Goldman held many minority opinions that others regarded with horror. In connection with religion, she maintained that puritanism is hypocrisy, that Christianity perpetuates slavery by offering poor people the promise of a prosperous afterlife, and that Zionism is a failed experiment in state control. It is doubtful whether any other atheists have shared all of her beliefs; it is likely that some atheists have disagreed with her about almost everything other than the non-existence of gods.

3.9 *A TWENTIETH-CENTURY BRITISH ATHEIST*

Eric Blair (1903–1950) was educated at St. Cyprians, where he became friends with Cyril Connelly, and at Eton, where he was taught French by Aldous Huxley. Between 1922 and 1927, he was a member of the Indian Imperial Police in Burma. After contracting dengue fever and returning to England, he resolved to become a writer. Between 1928 and 1932, he immersed himself in the world of the poor and downtrodden, and began to publish articles and essays based on this experience. He worked for two years as a teacher (1932–1933) and then for two years in a second-hand bookstore (1934–1935); during this period, under the pen-name 'George Orwell', he published *Down and Out in Paris and London* (1933), *Burmese Days* (1934), *A Clergyman's Daughter* (1935), and *Keep the Aspidistra Flying* (1936). After spending time researching social conditions in northern England, which provided the subject matter of *The Road to Wigan Pier* (1937), Blair married Eileen O'Shaughnessy, and set out for Spain, to fight with the Worker's Party of Marxist Unification, an adventure which provided material for *Homage to Catalonia* (1938). In Spain, Blair was shot in the throat, and his precarious health deteriorated; he convalesced in Morocco, using the time to write *Coming Up For Air* (1939) together with some of the essays included in *Inside the Whale* (1939). Blair's major wartime publications were *The Lion and the Unicorn: Socialism and the English Genius* (1941), and *Animal Farm* (1945). After the war, while fighting a losing battle with his health, Blair wrote *Nineteen Eighty-Four* (1949). He died in early 1950 at the age of forty-six.

Blair was eccentric in various ways. He was tall, gangly and uncoordinated; he was also socially awkward, with fairly narrow interests, and a monotonous voice. Throughout his life, he was a democratic socialist who had no time for authoritarianism and totalitarianism. While there are now people on the far right who claim Blair as one of their own, the sole explanation for this is that

Blair was the target of vicious Russian propaganda in the wake of his criticism of the behaviour of the International Brigades during the Spanish Civil War. While it seems that some people developed the idea that Blair was a 'secular saint', detailed critical scrutiny has brought to light less appealing aspects of his character. In many ways, he was a man of his time: he smoked heavily, he drank heavily, he was openly homophobic, he was openly anti-Semitic, he was a sexist 'womaniser', he had a penchant for beating his students, and he deliberately cultivated idiosyncrasies of manner and dress. He was also—perhaps in some mitigation of some of the foregoing—a victim of depression and ill-health who lived frugally and with little regard for his own well-being.

From the age of fourteen, Blair was an atheist who self-identified as a humanist. He was a stern critic of both religious teachings and religious organisations. He entirely rejected the idea that there is an afterlife, along with the idea that our universe is the product of the creative activities of a providential god. Moreover, he maintained that the Church of England is a selfish organisation devoted to serving the interests of the upper classes, completely out of touch with its lower-class membership, and an entirely pernicious influence on public life.

But, as in other respects, there was another side to Blair. Despite his avowed disdain for Christianity, Blair was a regular church attendee, to the point of continuing to take Communion. In a letter to Eleanor Jacques in 1932, he wrote:

> It seems rather mean to go to Holy Communion when one doesn't believe, but I have passed myself off for pious, and there is nothing for it but to keep up with the deception.
>
> (Orwell and Angus 1968: 271)

Moreover, he was twice married in Anglican churches, and wished to have an Anglican funeral. Nonetheless, in his review of *Critical Essays*, Evelyn Waugh (1946) says of Blair that 'he seems never to have been touched at any point by a conception of religious thought and life'. It is a plausible conjecture that Waugh would have supposed that the following passage—from Blair's essay 'Lear, Tolstoy and the Fool'—simply confirms his earlier observation:

Most people get a fair amount of fun out of their lives, but on balance life is suffering, and only the very young or the very foolish imagine otherwise. ... Ultimately, it is the Christian attitude which is self-interested and hedonistic, since the aim is always to get away from the painful struggle of earthly life and find eternal peace in some kind of heaven or nirvana. The humanist attitude is that the struggle must continue and that death is the price of life. ... Often there is a seeming truce between the humanist and the religious believer, but in fact their attitudes cannot be reconciled: one must choose between this world and the next. And the enormous majority of human beings, if they understand the issue, would choose this world. They do make the choice when the continue working, breeding and dying instead of crippling their faculties in the hope of obtaining a new lease of existence elsewhere.

(Orwell 1947: 429–430)

There is an interesting contrast in the attitudes towards religion of Mary Ann Evans and Eric Blair. Both are atheists; both think that religious teachings are all false. But, while Evans supposes that there is an important social function that is served by religion that might not be better served by anything else, it seems that Blair supposes that the social function of religion is in no better state than its doctrines: the false teachings of religion belong to institutions that benefit from their oppression of the poor and downtrodden. *And yet*: despite his wholly negative assessment of the teachings and social functions of religion, Blair continued to go to church and to participate in Communion. Was this really just, as Blair seems to suggest, a matter of keeping up social appearances? Was there some other kind of appreciation—perhaps an aesthetic resonance—with the rites and traditions of the Anglican Church? Was church attendance an opportunity for fieldwork, or perhaps down time in which the pressures of work were left behind? I have no idea.

3.10 *ANOTHER TWENTIETH-CENTURY BRITISH ATHEIST*

Margaret Kennedy (1903–1983) was born in Hertfordshire. She graduated from Girton College, Cambridge, in 1926, having finally, under the influence of her undergraduate lecturers, Russell, Broad, and McTaggart, abandoned the religious beliefs she had acquired during her childhood. Between 1926 and 1936, she was variously librarian, information officer, and editor for the house journal of the National Institute of Industrial Psychology. Following her marriage to Arthur Knight, she became an assistant lecturer in psychology at the University of Aberdeen. She was promoted to lecturer in 1948, and retired in 1970. Her major publications in psychology were a compilation of William James's writing on psychology—Knight (1950)—and a textbook—Knight and Knight (1948)—co-authored with Arthur, that ran through many subsequent editions.

Kennedy was a vocal proponent of scientific humanism; she achieved a level of notoriety in the UK when she gave two short radio talks on the BBC Home Service in 1955 under the title 'Morals without Religion'. These two talks, together with Kennedy's account of the response that they generated, and essays on other topics—evil, intuition, statistics and telepathy—of interest to her were published in Knight (1955). In subsequent years, she lectured widely on humanism, both in universities and at humanist events: for example, in 1957, she delivered the 48th Moncure Conway Memorial Lecture, on 'Physique and Personality', at an event chaired by Julian Huxley. Kennedy became an Honorary Associate of the Rationalist Press Association, and contributed to its journal, the *Humanist*. She edited an anthology on humanist thought (Knight 1961) and a response to Robinson (1963) with the title *Honest to Man* (Knight 1974).

When Kennedy first approached the BBC with scripts for her talks, they were rejected out of hand. However, she persisted, and was eventually permitted to give two talks on moral education for children of unbelievers. In the first talk, Kennedy argued that Christianity is not intellectually tenable, and the secular humanism provides a superior foundation for 'a constructive attitude to life and a code of conduct'. In the second talk, Kennedy discussed ways of bringing up children that conduce to the production of well-balanced, secure, affectionate and generous-minded adults, and suggests that, from a practical standpoint, we do not need to justify the fundamental moral axiom that we must not be completely selfish; that is, we must be prepared, at times and within limits, to put our own interests second to those of our family, or friends, or of the group or community to which we belong:

> I have never yet met the child—and I have met very few adults—to whom it has ever occurred to raise the question 'Why should I consider others?' Most people are prepared to accept as a completely self-evident moral axiom that we must not be completely selfish, and if we base our moral training on that we shall, I suggest, be building on firm enough foundations.
>
> (Knight 1955: 49)

The furore that erupted in response to Kennedy's talk was out of all proportion to their content. While we might now worry about her endorsement of corporal punishment, her over-heated fears about communism, and her focus on Christianity as *the* alternative to secular humanism, none of this was the focus of the UK press. The *Sunday Graphic* warned:

> Do not let this woman fool you. She looks—doesn't she—just like a typical housewife: cool, comfortable, harmless. But Mrs. Knight is a menace. A dangerous woman. Make no mistake about that.

The *Daily Express* cited the Archbishop of Canterbury, Dr Neville Gorton:

> This bossy female, this brusque, so-competent, bossy female. She seemed a very simple-minded female to me.

And the *Daily Telegraph* ran with the idea that the BBC was a sponsor of atheism, and that Kennedy's 'propaganda' was akin to:

> ... a serious apologia for polygamy, homosexuality, or any other manifestation of the frailties of human nature.

Privately, even the then Prime Minister—Winston Churchill—got in on the act, chastising the Director-General of the BBC for allowing Kennedy to 'pour out a selection of hackneyed assertions that must have caused pain to many people of all ages'.

Of course, not all of the responses to Kennedy's talks were negative; for example, Bertrand Russell wrote in her support (see Russell 1955). Perhaps ironically, but nonetheless understandably, the major consequence of the disproportionate response was a wave of criticism of religious broadcasting on the BBC that precipitated major reforms which broke down the virtual monopoly that religious believers had previously had for the broadcasting of their views (see Brown 2012).

While the views that Kennedy expressed in her 1955 talks seem quite mild, she went on to develop much stronger criticisms of Christianity in her subsequent publications. For example, in a short piece titled 'Christianity: The Debit Account' which was published in 1975, Kennedy argued against two beliefs that she had held at the time of the 1955 broadcasts, namely: that Jesus was a great moral teacher and a man of outstanding excellence, and that Christianity had been a great force for good in its day. After diligent study of the *Bible* and the origins and history of Christianity, Kennedy came to the view that Jesus was a fanatical idealist who could not tolerate disagreement and criticism, and that some of the worst features of life during the 'age of faith'—intolerance, persecution, anti-intellectualism, asceticism, otherworldliness, acceptance of the institution of slavery, and fear of eternal damnation—stemmed directly from the teachings of the churches. To take just one case: according to Kennedy, the abolitionist movement took its impetus from the secular humanitarianism of the Enlightenment; apart from the Quakers and a few like William Wilberforce, the attitude of the churches was, in the US, 'actively hostile', and, in the UK, in Wilberforce's own words, 'shamefully lukewarm'.

When Knight (1955) was published, Kennedy sent a copy to Bertrand Russell, with the inscription 'To Bertrand Russell with Gratitude'. Russell wrote a sympathetic response:

> I have been shocked but not surprised by the vehemence of the attacks on you. I keep a file labelled 'Christian Charity' of which I hope someday to make use in an essay called 'Christianity: The Religion of Love'.

> (Russell 1955: 223)

Alas, despite his own bulky file of letters from affronted Christians, Russell never got around to writing that essay. But Kennedy's response to her Christian critics in Knight (1955) goes some way towards filling that void.

3.11 A TWENTY-FIRST-CENTURY IRANIAN ATHEIST

Maryam Namazie (1966–) was born in Tehran, but emigrated with her family after the Iranian Revolution. She is a prominent human rights activist and secularist who values political *ideals* above political *identities*.

In the late 1980s, Namazie worked with Ethiopian refugees in Sudan. In 1991, she was co-founder of the Committee for Humanitarian Assistance to Iranian Refugees. In 1994, she worked in, and produced a film about, Iranian refugee camps in Turkey. After her election as Executive Director of the International Federation of Iranian Refugees and Immigrant Councils in the mid-1990s, she led campaigns against human rights violations of refugees in Turkey. Since 1996, she has also been a spokesperson for Equal Rights Now, an organisation that opposes discrimination against women in Iran, and, since 2009, she has been a spokesperson for Iran Solidarity, an organisation that opposes the Islamic regime in Iran. Namazie has led the Council of Ex-Muslims of Britain since its inception in 2007, and has been a spokesperson for One Law for All—a campaign against local sharia law in the UK—since its launch in 2008. In 2012, she became a patron of London Black Atheists; she is also a patron of Pink Triangle Trust. Since 2013, she has been spokesperson for Fitnah: Movement for Women's Liberation, which opposes misogynistic cultural, religious and moral laws and customs, compulsory veiling, sex apartheid, sex trafficking, and violence against women. Namazie is a member of the Worker-Communist Party of Iran, and editor of its journal, the *Worker-Communist Review*; she is also a member of the International Committee against Stoning.

Namazie has been involved in many controversies. She was one of twelve signatories to *Manifesto: Together Facing the New Totalitarianism*, a response to the Danish cartoon crisis of 2005–2006. She was one of fifty-five signatories to an open letter in *The Guardian* that opposed a state visit to the UK by Pope Benedict XVI. As a keynote speaker at the World Atheist Convention in 2011, she denounced the 'Islamic Inquisition', and called for people to stop using the term 'Islamophobia'. In 2012, she launched a calendar of naked female activists. Since 2014, with Fariborz Pooya, Namazie has co-hosted a weekly bilingual—English and Farzi—TV broadcast, *Bread and Roses*, which addresses apostasy, blasphemy, LGBT rights, secularism, sharia law, women unveiling, and a host of other controversial topics, and which has been roundly condemned by the Islamic Republic of Iran. In 2015, the Warwick University Student Union blocked an event, organised by the Warwick Atheists, Secularists and Humanists, at which Namazie was to speak, and a talk that she gave at Goldsmiths University degenerated into a slanging match between the speaker and members of the Goldsmith University Islamic Society.

An important strand in Namazie's thought focuses on a 'fault-line' in attitudes towards 'minorities within minorities' in prosperous democracies:

> Many secularists in Europe have shown a lack of clarity and moral courage when it comes to banning the burqa and niqab. Secularism ... is a fundamental precondition for women's rights and equality. Secularists have a responsibility to seize the initiative, particularly given the far-Right's attempts at hijacking the issue to promote anti-immigrant and anti-Muslim bigotry. ... A ban has nothing to do with a 'clash of civilisations'; it has everything to do with a global struggle between secularists, including many Muslims, on the one hand, and theocrats and the religious Right on the other.
>
> (Namazie undated)

> Sometimes, where we're having these discussions, people only see homogeneous groups; they make decisions based on group identity. But group identity is very often imposed. It fails to recognise that there are so many individuals within these groups who are ... courageously resisting in many different ways, often at great risk to themselves. ... It is important for us to go back to basic human rights, citizenship, and secularism, and to join hands together around political ideals and not identities.
>
> (Namazie, cited in Jacobsen 2016)

> When you side with identity politics and homogenised communities, you end up siding with ... the ruling class, and never with dissenters. Identity politics sees only homogenised culture and religion as [endorsed] by the gatekeepers of power. Identity politics misses class politics, and internal political and social movements.
>
> (Namazie, cited in Sporenda 2017)

In his defence of those who blocked Namazie's talk at Warwick University, Shariatmadari (2015) writes:

> What might lead people to decide they'd rather not give a platform to such rhetoric? Recognising the pressure British Muslims are under—surveilled by the state, victims of verbal abuse, vandalism and arson—could it be that some students felt welcoming a person who believes that Islam is incompatible with modern life would be wrong? ... The underlying sentiment is reasonable: we don't want to have any part in the future stigmatisation of Islam. ... We are lucky to live in a pluralist democracy, with freedom of choice in politics and religion. These are things we should cherish, but they are not in any serious danger. Were they really threatened ... the left would resist with every sinew. I hope that more citizens in Muslim-majority countries can one day enjoy the level of political and social freedom that we do, and I support the men and women who try to bring that about.

I think that it would be reasonable for Namazie to point out that much of her life's work has been devoted to trying to make it the case that more citizens in Muslim-majority countries—and more dissenting Muslims in Muslim-minority countries—enjoy basic social and religious freedoms. While Shariatmadari is right in thinking that, in early twenty-first century Britain, *his* freedom of social—and religious and political—choice is not in any serious danger, it is not nearly so clear that, at this time, the freedom of social—and religious and political—choice of *dissenting Muslims* is similarly fortunately placed. Of course, Shariatmadari is right to insist on opposition to abuse, arson, vandalism, improper state surveillance, and everything else that puts *all* Muslims under pressure; but surely this opposition can be managed in a nuanced way that does not throw dissenting Muslims—whose efforts elsewhere in the world receive Shariatmadari's endorsement—under the bus.

3.12 A TWENTY-FIRST-CENTURY GHANAIAN ATHEIST

Agomo Atambire (1989–) is an atheist who lives in Accra, Ghana. He calls himself 'a freethinking humanist big-mouthed non-Westerner' and claims that his profession 'ranges between freelance journalist, entrepreneur, and professional troublemaker'. Atambire is from a very small ethnic group—the Frafra—in northern Ghana. He is a graduate of the University for Development Studies in Tamala, and holds a Bachelor of Science in Agricultural Technology with a major in Biotechnology. Atambire is the Organising Secretary of the Humanist Association of Ghana. During 2016, while he was a trainee with *fluter.de* in Berlin, he wrote a number of interesting columns comparing life in Berlin with life in Accra. He has also written some short pieces on genetically modified foods, the G20 protests, climate change, and challenges to those who believe in spirits, demons and dwarves.

The first face-to-face meeting of freethinkers in Ghana was held in Accra in 2012; it was organised by a network of freethinkers that emerged on social media. The Humanist Association of Ghana became an officially registered body in 2015. Its official aims are to promote critical thinking and humanism, and to agitate for human rights: 'We believe we can create a better society through discussion and action based on science, reason, and respect for human dignity.' In slightly more detail, the Humanist Association of Ghana aims to:

- promote an ethical life based on reason and human values;
- support human rights in the belief that all people are worthy of respect as long as they are not infringing on the rights or well-being of others;
- promote science and critical thinking as the primary ways to understand the world;
- transcend divisive loyalties based on race, religion, gender, politics, nationality, class and ethnicity;
- support an open, pluralistic and diverse society;
- support a secular government that guarantees freedom of religion for all;
- provide a support network for those who have no religious beliefs or wish to question their own received assumptions;

- promote separation of religion and state; and
- work with all individuals and organisation that share these concern.

In 2012, when the seeds of the Humanist Association of Ghana were being sown, a WIN–Gallup International Poll found that, while 96 per cent of Ghanaians claimed to be religious, fully 0 per cent of Ghanaians claimed to be atheists. The group currently has about 40 members, mostly aged between 23 and 35, and a quarter of whom are women. Almost all of them grew up in religious families, but became atheists in response to the unfolding of their lives.

Atambire (2014) describes his visit to 'a traditional African priest' who, his friends surmise, can provide him with evidence that will push him back into the 'light of faith'. Atambire notes that the Frafras are particularly superstitious, that he was named in honour of one of the traditional gods, and that he has long been an atheist. Although he meets with the priest a number of times, he is presented with tricks and evasion, but not with any reason to believe in spirits, demons, dwarves, or gods. His closing challenge, to all theistic readers—of whatever persuasion—is either to pony up the evidence or else to stop handing on hearsay stories that are passed from generation to generation in the absence of any compelling reasons to accept them.

In his piece on the G20 protests, Atambire writes:

> As Non-Westerners, the demonstrations give us mixed feelings. ... We are like people whose limbs have been cut off by the West: should we be consoled when we are thrown some prosthetic limbs in the form of 'solidarity'. Solidarity without a power shift? You know we cannot cash that cheque. Good intentions alone do us no good. ... Who knows, maybe the protests were more about a particular orange personality with small hands and a large mouth. Perhaps the demonstrations were more concerned with polar bears and climate disaster ...; after all, polar bears are closer neighbours than developing countries. Don't get me wrong, I love those cute ice bastards too, it's just that our pressing climate issues are problems concerning the whole of humanity. But, if we removed these 'Western problems' from the agenda, how many people would be

left to demonstrate in solidarity with the exploited developing nations? ... To Western youth today: your actions are laudable but we await proof of your commitment in the future. Please don't disappoint us.

(Atambire 2017b)

To take an example that Atambire himself does not consider, Australia's ratio of aid to gross national income hit an all-time low of 0.22 in 2016–2017. In real terms, Australia's aid budget of $3.8 billion in 2016–2017 was a third less than the $5.1 billion spent in 2012–2013. While, in the past decade, both sides of Australian politics have made verbal commitments to meet an aid-to-gross-national-income ratio of 0.5—still well below the UN target of 0.7 which, in 2015, was met or exceeded only by Denmark, Norway, Sweden, The Netherlands, Luxemburg and the UK—neither side has turned those commitments into action. While this is but one straw in the wind, it is a fair indication that it would be unwise for Atambire to hold his breath.

Atambire's pieces on genetically modified organisms—Atambire (2016; 2017a)—take issue with the anti-GMO campaign of Food Sovereignty Ghana. Atambire argues: that there is no evidence that GMOs are unsafe for human consumption; that—like climate change deniers and anti-vaxxers—FSG falsely denies that there is a scientific consensus about the safety of GMOs; that FSG's acceptance of the decades-old practice of using genetically engineered insulin in the treatment of diabetes shows that FSG operates according to a double standard; and that, in the face of the army worm infestation in Southern Africa—not to mention the need to increase yields, reduce use of pesticides and fertiliser, and deal with the prolonged droughts that will follow in the wake of global warming—the development of GMOs is our best bet for enabling food security in the region in the long run.

According to AFP (2016), death threats are an accepted part of Atambire's life, not because of his controversial views about GMOs and the G20 protests, but because of his atheism. In the early twenty-first century, Ghanaian atheists face social isolation, disownment by former friends and family members, and much worse. They, too, could do with something more than mere Western 'solidarity'.

3.13 *A CONCLUDING OBSERVATION*

Almost everything that is written about the lives of individual atheists focuses on the lives of those who belong to social elites (i.e. those with social privilege, influence, power, money, and the like). Even if we consider the broader sweep of those who *lack* belief in gods, we find very few works that discuss the belief and values of non-elite members of this category. Budd (1977) examines long-term and leading members of secular organisations between 1850 and 1960, with a particular focus on the period between 1870 and 1910, drawing from obituaries in the journals of these organisations; this is obviously a very small corner of the world of non-elite non-believers. And Sheard (2014) makes an interesting small-sample study of 'atheism and atheisation' on the part of 'ordinary people' in the UK—drawing upon oral history archives in which 'ordinary people' happen to make disclosures about their 'atheism and atheisation'—but notes that there is much more to be done to build adequate knowledge even of 'atheism and atheisation' in twenty-first-century Britain. That's about it.

FACTS AND FIGURES

There are lots of questions about atheists that we might hope to answer using the techniques of the social sciences.

The questions that we ask might be *global*—they might concern atheists the world over—or they might be *local*—they might concern atheists in particular regions: neighbourhoods, cities, states, countries, continents, trading blocs, etc.

The questions that we ask might be *synchronic*—they might concern atheists at a particular point in time, often enough, the present—or they might be *diachronic*: they might ask after respects in which atheists, or populations of atheists, change over time.

As we shall see, there are difficulties that confront all attempts to obtain accurate past and current information about atheists.

4.1 *COUNTING ATHEISTS*

Perhaps the most fundamental social scientific questions about atheists are *numerical*: How many atheists are there now? How many atheists were there in the past? What percentage of people in a given population are atheists? What percentage of people in a given population at a given point in history were atheists? How is the percentage of atheists in a given population changing over time?

You might think that it can't be hard to answer these questions. We have census data: most countries ask for information about religious orientation in their national census. And we have survey data: there are various organisations—Pew, WIN-Gallup, etc.—that collect and analyse global information about religious orientation. Moreover, these data are readily available on the Internet, where conclusions based upon the data are often presented as transparently factual.

Consider, for example, Vogt (2016), who tells us that, based on data collected by CARA—the Centre for Applied Research in the Apostolate, a national non-profit research group associated with Georgetown University—7 per cent of Americans say that God does not exist, and 17 per cent say that they do not believe in God. CARA asked respondents to select which one of the following five claims best fit them:

- I believe in God and have no doubt of God's existence.
- I believe in God but sometimes have doubts that God exists.
- I believe in God but have frequent doubts that God exists.
- I don't believe in God but still believe it is possible that God may exist.
- I don't believe in God. I am entirely sure God does not exist.

The first and last options are naturally read as statements about *conviction*: I am certain that God exists; I am certain that God does not exist. The second and third options are naturally read as statements about *fluctuations in belief*: sometimes, my belief that God exists wavers; often, my belief in God wavers. And the fourth option is naturally read as a statement about *(dominant) belief*: I believe that it is possible that God exists (although I don't believe that God exists). However, if we are genuinely interested in mapping a spectrum of attitudes, then the very first requirement is that our questions should be *even-handed* and *symmetrical* across opposing positions. For each of the first three questions, there are two 'opposing' options that can be offered:

- I don't believe in God and have no doubt of God's non-existence.
- I believe that God does not exist, and have no doubt of God's non-existence.
- I don't believe in God but sometimes have doubts that God does not exist.
- I believe that God does not exist, but sometimes have doubts that God does not exist.

- I don't believe in God but have frequent doubts that God does not exist.
- I believe that God does not exist, but have frequent doubts that God does not exist.

And for the last two questions, there is an 'opposing' option that can be offered:

- I believe in God but still believe it is possible that God may not exist.
- I believe in God. I am entirely sure that God does exist.

Given the initial set of five statements, and given the two options made available to those who do not wish to affirm any of the first three statements, it is clear that we simply cannot get accurate information about who believes that God does not exist and who merely fails to believe that God exists from this question set. Suppose that I believe that God does not exist, that I am not prone to episodes of doubt about God's non-existence, and that I nonetheless maintain an appropriate degree of doxastic humility in my believing, so that I will not accept that I am certain that God exists. Which box should I tick? The only plausible option is the fourth box. But, given my beliefs, I'm not one of those who merely fails to believe that God does not exist.

Problems in the formulation of posed questions arise even in connection with questionnaires developed by large polling organisations. Consider the question that was set by WIN-Gallup International as the basis for its Global Index of Religiosity and Atheism:

> Irrespective of whether you attend a place of worship or not, would you say you are a religious person, not a religious person, or a convinced atheist?

On the basis of responses to this question, we are told that 59 per cent of the world says that they are religious, 23 per cent say that they are not religious, and 13 per cent say that they are convinced atheists. But the choice of categories here is bizarre. First of all, 'religious'/'not religious' is binary: everyone falls on one side or the other of this divide (I leave to one side any considerations about the possibility of 'borderline' cases). Second, 'convinced atheists' can belong to either of these categories: some convinced atheists are religious, and some—plausibly many more—convinced atheists are not religious. Since we have no way of knowing how people decided to sort themselves into these categories, it is not clear that there is anything that we can safely conclude about the global prevalence of atheism from the data collected in this poll. Perhaps you might say: surely we can conclude that, on this data, *at least* 13 per cent of the population of the world are atheists. But even that's not obvious. It depends, among other things, on how the expression 'convinced atheist' was understood by those taking the poll. Suppose, for example, that I take 'atheist' to denote those who fail to believe that there are gods, and suppose that I am a resolute agnostic: I am firm in my suspension of judgment on the question whether there are gods. Does that make me a 'convinced atheist'? Plausibly, yes. So, even given the data, it's not clear that we're licensed in drawing the conclusion that at least 13 per cent of the population of the world are atheists.

Problems about the formulation of the questions to ask when polling people to determine whether they are atheists do not exhaust the difficulties to be confronted. If we are designing new polls, aimed at collecting information about the current distribution of atheists, we may need to worry about: (a) the different ways in which different populations understand the term 'atheist' and related expressions in other languages; (b) the different ways in which different populations understand other key terms—'God', 'religious', 'belief', and so on—and related expressions in other languages that are used in the formulation of these questions; (c) the fact that some people have confused or incoherent beliefs about atheism, perhaps because they have confused or incoherent understanding of the term 'atheism' and related and related expressions in other languages; (d) the fact that, in almost every country, the term 'atheist', or its counterparts in other languages, is associated with social stigma, discrimination and persecution, which gives motivation to some atheists to hide their atheism; (e) the fact that, while, in some countries, governments promote atheism, in other countries, governments oppose atheism, and in yet other countries, at least 'officially', governments are neutral with respect to atheism; and (f) the fact that there is not always consistency between what people say and what they do: some people claim to be—or to have been—atheists even though their behaviour, or the record of their behaviour, says otherwise; and some people claim not to be—or not to have been—atheists, even though their behaviour, or the record of their behaviour, says otherwise. Moreover, if we are relying upon polling that was carried out in earlier times, then, in addition to variants of all of the worries just mentioned, we also need to worry about the fact that the framing of the relevant questions—in, for example, national censuses—varies greatly over time: the questions that were used to elicit information about atheists in the 1920s are very different from the questions that are now used to elicit information about atheists.

Some of the difficulties that we have just mentioned can be overcome. Gervais and Najile (2017) used an unmatched count technique and Bayesian estimation to determine the prevalence of those who fail to believe that God exists in the US. They worked with two nationally representative samples of two thousand American Adults provided to them by YouGov, an organisation that specialises in the provision of omnibus nationally representative polling.

The first sample were uniformly assigned to one of three conditions: a third were asked to say *how many* of nine 'innocuous' statements were not true of them (e.g. 'I own a dog', 'I have a dishwasher in my kitchen', etc.); a third were asked to say *how many* of ten statements were not true of them, where the ten statements were the previously mentioned nine plus 'I believe in God'; and a third self-reported whether or not the claim 'I believe in God' was true of them.

The second sample were uniformly assigned to one of three conditions: a third were asked to say *how many* of six 'innocuous' statements were true of them; a third were asked to say *how many* of seven statements were true of them, where the seven statements were the previously mentioned six together with 'I do not believe in God'; and a third were asked to say how many of seven statements were true of them, where the seven statement were the previously mentioned six together with 'I do not believe that two plus two is less than thirteen'.

Roughly speaking, analysis of the first sample suggested that 32 per cent of Americans do not believe in God, and analysis of the second sample suggested that 20 per cent of Americans do not believe in God; whence analysis of the two samples together suggested that 26 per cent of Americans do not believe in God. (Why are the results of the two samples different? Gervais and Najile suggest that it might be because of difference in response to positive versus negative framing of the key statement: 'I believe in God' versus 'I do not believe in God'. Given the size of the effect, it would be nice to know whether we have reason to suppose that one framing yields more reliable results than the other.) Interestingly—and very puzzlingly—the final third of the second sample reported more statements were true of them than did the first third; this might seem to raise serious questions about the reliability of the entire experimental set-up. But Gervais and Najile nonetheless insist that we can be more or less certain that there are many more Americans who fail to believe that God exists than any telephone polls have hitherto suggested.

Gervais and Najile use the term 'atheist' to refer to people who fail to believe that God exists. They say that this usage is standard in the psychology, sociology and philosophy of religion, and that it is the definition that is adopted in the *Oxford English Dictionary*. While they may be right about usage in the psychology and sociology of religion, it is worth noting that their method could easily be adapted to investigate what percentage of people believe that there is no God. In the second sample, instead of 'I do not believe in God', we could add 'I believe that there is no God' to the questions for the middle third; and, in the first sample, we could replace 'I believe in God' with 'I believe there is no God' for the middle third (and perhaps adjust the other questions so that they also involve a negative element—e.g. 'I have never attended a professional soccer match'). Given that theists are those who believe that there is at least one god, and atheists are those who believe that there are no gods, any method that can identify those who are not theists (i.e. those who lack the belief that there is at least one god) can readily be adapted to identify those who are not atheists (i.e. those who lack the belief that there are no gods; and in this second case, of course, those who are left over are the atheists).

While, in principle, it is clear that we could find out how many people are atheists, in practice there has never been any enthusiasm for this task. There is no census form for any country that has a box 'I believe that there are no gods'. Similarly, in all large scale social scientific surveys, there is no box on the survey form for 'I believe that there are no gods'. I do not see any good reason for having this state of affairs continue.

4.2 STEREOTYPING ATHEISTS

> The Fool says in his heart 'There is no God'. They are corrupt, they do abominable deeds, there is none that does good.
>
> (Psalms 14:1)

Stereotypes of atheists agree with the Psalmist. Among widely shared stereotypical beliefs about atheists, there are at least the following:

- Atheists are untrustworthy.
- Atheists break the law.
- Atheists are immoral.
- Atheists have no values.
- Atheists don't believe in anything.
- Atheists are selfish.
- Atheists are unhappy.
- Atheists are emotionally unstable.
- Atheists have mental health problems.
- Atheists are sexually deviant.
- Atheists are physically unhealthy.
- Atheists have low life expectancy.

As we have already noted, the exact content of these stereotypes is not obvious. While the Psalmist clearly does have atheists—those who believe that there are no gods—in mind, others are likely to have a broader target that includes all of those who fail to believe that there are gods, those who fail to believe that there is exactly one god, and perhaps even those who fail to believe in 'the one true god'. For the purposes of the coming discussion, I shall often assume that, where social scientific studies have used the term 'atheist' to cover those who fail to believe that there are gods, the results of those studies carry over to the narrower class of what I call 'atheists' (i.e. those who believe that there are no gods). However, there are some cases where there is reason to be very cautious about such extrapolation.

4.2.1 UNTRUSTWORTHINESS

Stereotyping atheists as untrustworthy has a distinguished pedigree. In 1689, John Locke—in his *Letter Concerning Toleration*—wrote:

> Those are not at all to be tolerated who deny the Being of a God. Promises, Covenants, and Oaths, which are the Bonds of Humane Society, can have no hold upon an Atheist.

(Locke 1689/1983: 52)

I take it that Locke's thought is something like this. When one theist makes a promise to a second theist, both believe that God witnesses the making of the promise, and both believe that God will not be pleased if the promise is broken; consequently, the one to whom the promise is made can be confident that the other will keep the promise, and the one making the promise has very strong incentive to keep the promise. But, if an atheist makes a 'promise' to a theist, the atheist believes neither that God witnesses the making of the 'promise' nor that God will be displeased if the 'promise' is broken; whence, it seems, Locke supposes that the atheist has no reason to keep the 'promise' and the theist has no reason to suppose that the atheist will keep the 'promise'.

Gervais, Norenzayan and Shariff (2011) argue that distrust is central to anti-atheist prejudice. In a series of experiments, they show that: (a) anti-atheist prejudice is characterised by distrust whereas anti-gay prejudice is characterised by disgust; (b) descriptions of untrustworthy people are viewed as representative of atheists; and (c) anti-atheist prejudice is stronger in contexts in which trust is salient. Gervais et al. claim that we can explain anti-atheist prejudice by appealing to two important truths: (1) religions have played significant roles in enabling social coordination and social cooperation in human societies, and (2) atheists are viewed as significant potential disrupters that could prevent religion from successfully playing those roles. Given that religions have facilitated social cohesion, coordination and cooperation in human societies by 'outsourcing social monitoring and punishment to supernatural agents'—as per my gloss on the above quote from Locke—it is to be expected that religiosity is viewed as a proxy for trustworthiness, and that the lack of religiosity evidenced by atheists is taken to signal untrustworthiness.

Gervais et al. rely on the conjunction fallacy paradigm. Tversky and Kahneman (1983) found that participants given a description of an outspoken and politically active single woman often judged that it is more likely that the woman is a bank teller *and* a feminist than that she is a bank teller. But the probability of a conjunction cannot be higher than the probability of any of its conjuncts: it cannot be that it is more likely that one is a feminist bank teller than that one is a bank teller. The standard explanation for this result is that people often rely on the heuristic judgment that the description makes the woman sound like a feminist.

Gervais et al. gave their participants a description of a person who commits a variety of selfish and illegal acts in circumstances where those acts will almost certainly go undetected and then—for different uniform samples from their participants—elicited judgments about whether it is more likely that the person is a teacher or more likely that the person is a teacher *and* an atheist/rapist/Christian/Muslim. They found that propensity to make the conjunction fallacy was significantly higher—for all kinds of participants—when the conjunction was *teacher and atheist* than when it was *teacher and Christian* or *teacher and Muslim*. The standard explanation says that participants often rely on the heuristic judgment that the description—as atheist—makes the person sound untrustworthy.

Other studies of atheism and trustworthiness use different paradigms. Tan and Vogel (2008) examined behaviour in computerised economic trust games in which participants are provided with information about a potential trustee's religiosity. They found that both trust and trustworthiness increased with a potential trustee's religiosity, and that they increased more in proportion to the trustee's greater religiosity.

The participants in the study of Tan and Vogel played two stages in their game, using uniform sampling to determine which stage given participants played first. In the *proposer* stage, each player had twenty-six turns. Each turn, they were given ten 50-cent coins with the free option of passing on some of the coins to another person, who receives three times the number of coins passed on. After the first turn, the proposer was given a piece of information about the receiver, concerning religious orientation, or environmental friendliness, or political inclination, or social attitude. In the *responder* stage, each player had ten turns. In each turn, the player had to say how much they would pass back to the sender for each possible amount they might receive. Participants in the study were paid eight dollars for undertaking an initial questionnaire—which elicited information about religious orientation, etc.—and earned money from their participation in the game according to uniform matching, with participants who fit the relevant information as determined by the initial questionnaire, on uniformly sampled turns.

Unlike Gervais, Norenzayan and Shariff (2011), Tan and Vogel (2008) found that those with low religiosity were not more inclined to trust those with higher religiosity; in addition, they also found that those with higher religiosity were more likely to be trusting (i.e. more likely to reward those who 'invested' in them).

The question whether religion promotes trust is sensitive to considerations about exactly what trusting behaviour requires. Sosis (2005) works with the proposal that one person trusts another if the first acts in the expectation that the second will perform a particular action when the following two conditions hold: (a) both know that, if the second fails to perform the action in question, then the first would have been better off not to perform the original action; and (b) both know that the first person's acting as they do gives the second person a reason not to perform the action in question. On the basis of this analysis of trusting action, Sosis argues that, while there is no need for trusting behaviour in closed religious communities, religious practices and symbolic markers are successful in promoting trust among in-group members and anonymous co-religionists in situations in which social groups are fluid; and he notes further that religious badges of identity can be used by non-group members as symbols of trustworthiness. Sosis's claims are consistent with the results of both Tan and Vogel (2008) and Gervais, Norenzayan and Shariff (2011).

Many studies in the US—and elsewhere—confirm the results of the studies that we have considered: there is very widespread distrust of atheists that manifests in various kinds of prejudicial behaviour in connection with, for example, elections to public office, employment, family life and social inclusion.

4.2.2 CRIMINALITY

The widespread stereotyping of atheists as untrustworthy does not occur in a vacuum: if atheists are untrustworthy, then there are reasons why atheists are untrustworthy. One common reason for thinking that atheists are untrustworthy is that they have greater than usual propensity to engage in criminal activity.

The relationship between religiosity and criminality has been much studied. While the outcomes have been mixed—some studies have found no relationship between religiosity and crime, and others have found differing degrees to which religiosity moderates criminal offending—there is a broad consensus in the social scientific literature that there is a genuine correlation between increasing religious involvement and decreasing criminality.

Hoskin et al. (2017) conducted a study of college students in the United States and Malaysia. They surveyed 1359 Malaysian undergraduates and 1629 US undergraduates. They collected self-reported data about *criminal involvement*—bodily assault, sexual assault, domestic violence, theft, property damage, reckless driving, bribery, fraud, distribution of illegal drugs, use of illegal drugs, and illegal gambling; *religiosity*—strictness of parental enforcement of religious teachings, importance attributed to religion, activity in religious observance, obedience to specific religious teachings, degree of fundamentalism, belief in God and belief in immortality; and *control factors*—age, sex, Chinese ancestry, marital status of parents, closeness to family, academic performance, level of self-control, openness to risk and level of alcohol consumption. Analysis of the collected date for amount and spread ('versatility') of criminal behaviour led Hoskin et al. to conclude that alcohol consumption and religiosity were the only significant factors among those studied that contributed to the greatly reduced criminality of Malaysian students in comparison to US students. While, as always, there are limitations of this study (e.g. the sample is college students, there are legal differences between the US and Malaysia, there are weaknesses in the reliability of self-report, and so on), Hoskin et al. end their paper with the confident assertion that 'studies like the present one will inform strategies that look to religious involvement as a way to reduce criminality, not only in the US but in other societies as well'.

The final conclusion drawn by Hoskin et al. is evidently premature. Criminality is only one among various characteristics that vary with religiosity; whether we should look to religious involvement as a way to reduce criminality depends upon what else comes along with religious involvement. More importantly, even if there were nothing else that varied with religiosity, the study by Hoskin et al. simply does not support the conclusion that they draw. As Schroeder, Broadus and Bradley (2017) have noted, studies like the one conducted by Hoskin et al. do not pay attention to the distinction between non-believers who have a strong social identity and non-believers who do not have a strong social identity.

In their own study, working with survey information from 643 undergraduates at a university in the US Midwest, Schroeder et al. analysed data about *religious belief*—'atheist' ('I don't believe in God'), 'agnostic' ('I don't know whether there is a God and I don't believe there is any way to find out'), 'higher power' ('I don't believe in a personal God but I do believe in a Higher Power'), '50/50' ('I find myself believing in God some of the time but not others'), 'questioning' ('While I have doubts, I feel that I do believe in God'), and 'believer' ('I know God really exists and I have no doubts about it'); *religiosity*—church attendance, prayer frequency, and importance attributed to religion; *criminal involvement*—drug and alcohol use, property damage, theft, assault, and drug dealing; and *control factors*—age, sex, race, income, education, rurality, relationship status, and religious denomination. For the purposes of their analysis, the used a three-point scheme of classification: non-believers ('atheists' and 'agnostics'), uncertain believers ('higher power', '50/50', and 'questioning'), and certain believers ('believers'). They found that, while non-believers and certain believers offend at similar rates, uncertain believers offend at significantly higher rates. According to Schroeder et al. the existing consensus is mistaken: religiosity itself is not related to general criminal offending.

After recognising the various limitations of their study—e.g. that it does not include any direct measures for social control and social identity, that it uses a sample of predominantly Christian US college students, and that the cross-sectional analysis that it employs cannot definitely establish causal ordering—Schroeder et al. hypothesise that, unlike certain believers and non-believers, uncertain believers fail to benefit from strong group identification, and that this explains their greater criminality and deviance. Whether or not this is correct, it is clear that further research on the question of religiosity and crime must pay attention to the distinction between 'non-believers' and 'uncertain believers'. Rather than follow Hoskin et al. in supposing that we need strategies that look to religious involvement as way to reduce criminality, we might do better to suppose that we need strategies that look to strong group identification as a way of reducing criminality. Certainly, given the current state of social scientific research on religiosity and criminality, the social scientific literature gives us no reason at all to suppose that atheists—in the US or elsewhere in the world—have a greater propensity to engagement in criminal activity than those in other 'religious' groupings.

Some people have supposed that data about incarceration rates support the conclusion that atheists have a lower propensity to engage in criminal activity than the rest of the population. Mehta (2015) reports that just 0.1 per cent of the US Federal prison population are atheists; the UK 2011 Census tells us that just 0.2 per cent of the UK prisoners are atheists. In both cases, we seem to see a significant under-representation of atheist prisoners. But there are many variables (e.g. income, race, and residency status) that are correlated with both atheism and rates of incarceration; and there are the usual issues about the reliability of self-reports of religious identification. While it seems clear that data about incarceration rates do nothing to support stereotypes about atheist criminality, it might be rash to conclude that the data we have actually indicate lower rates of criminality among atheists.

4.2.3 IMMORALITY

The stereotyping of atheists as having a greater propensity to engage in criminal activity fits with a broader stereotyping of atheists as having a greater propensity to engage in immoral behaviour.

In a recently conducted study, Gervais et al. (2017) examined intuitive judgments about the immorality of atheists across a range of nations: Australia, China, Czech Republic, Finland, Hong Kong, India, Mauritius, Netherlands, New Zealand, Singapore, UAE, UK, and USA. This study relied on the conjunction fallacy paradigm. In the main part of the study, participants were asked to read a description of a man who tortures small animals as a child, and then, as an adult, exhibits escalating violence that culminates in the murder and mutilation of five homeless people. Some uniformly selected participants were asked to judge whether it is more probable that the man is a teacher or a teacher who does not believe in God; and the remaining uniformly selected participants were asked to judge whether it is more probable that the man is a teacher or a teacher who is a religious believer. Gervais et al. used the generated information about conjunction fallacy rates to determine the degree to which the description fits with stereotypes of believers and non-believers.

In order to check for confounds and alternative explanations, Gervais et al. also conducted three supplementary studies. In the first supplementary study, the description concerned a minor moral violation, e.g. not paying for dinner at a restaurant. (Different descriptions were used in different countries to accommodate differences in views about what counts as a minor moral violation.) In the second supplementary study, which used the same description as the main study, participants were variously asked to judge whether it is more probable that the man is a teacher *or*: (a) a teacher who does not believe in God; (b) a teacher who does not believe in evolution; (c) a teacher who does not believe in the accuracy of horoscopes; (d) a teacher who does not believe in the reality of global warming; (e) a teacher who does not believe in the safety of vaccines. In the third supplementary study, the description concerned a priest who had been molesting young boys for decades, and participants were asked to judge whether it is more likely that the priest believes in God or that the priest does not believe in God.

Upon analysis of the data, Gervais et al. found that, overall, people are twice as likely to view extreme immorality as representative of atheists relative to religious believers. Interestingly, they found that *even atheists* intuitively associate serial murder more with atheists than with religious believers. Moreover, by considerations of the data from the supplementary studies, Gervais et al. found that these results hold up for minor moral misdemeanours, are not attributable to prejudice against general lack of belief, and persist even for moral violations that might intuitively be associated with particular religious groups (e.g. paedophile priests). According to Gervais et al., their results show that, worldwide, religious belief is taken to be a bulwark against the temptations of immoral conduct, and that, again worldwide, atheists are broadly taken to be dangerously morally depraved. While Gervais et al. do note that there are countries (e.g. Finland and New Zealand) in which this kind of anti-atheist prejudice is less pronounced, they suggest that widespread intuitive moral suspicion of atheists is a barrier to their 'full acceptance' in many societies.

Some people have supposed that we might defend the view that atheists are morally *superior* to religious believers by examining cross-national correlations between religiosity and psychosociological well-being. For example, Paul (2009) examines the relationship between religiosity and psychosociological condition in some prosperous democracies: Australia, Austria, Canada, Denmark, England, France, Germany, Holland, Ireland, Italy, Japan, New Zealand, Norway, Spain, Sweden, Switzerland, and the United States. His measure of *religiosity* is based on data in seven categories: percentage of population that is certain that God exists; percentage of population that are Biblical literalists; percentage of population that regularly attends religious services; percentage of population that prays regularly; percentage of population that believes in an afterlife; percentage of population that are atheists and agnostics; and percentage of population that accepts common ancestry of humans and other animals. After normalisation on a 0–10 scale, with 0 for the most religious score and 10 for the most secular score in each category, an unweighted mean is calculated for each nation: its *religiosity score*. Paul's measure of *psychosociological condition* is based on data in twenty-five categories: per capita homicide rates; per capita incarceration rates; per capita juvenile mortality; average lifespan; per capita adolescent gonorrhoea and syphilis infections; per capita all age gonorrhoea and syphilis infections; per capita adolescent abortions; per capita adolescent births; per capita youth suicide; per capita all age suicide; per capita fertility; per capita marriage; per capita marriage duration; per capita divorce; average life satisfaction; per capita alcohol consumption; national corruption; per capita income; national income disparity; national rates of poverty; national employment rate; per capita hours of work; and per capita resource exploitation base. After normalisation on a 0–10 scale, with 0 for the worst case and 10 for the best case in each category, an unweighted mean is calculated for each nation: its *societal success score*. Plotting the societal success score against the religiosity score yields a graphic depiction of the relationship that holds between national religiosity and national psychosociological well-being. Table 4.1 shows Paul's results.

I have divided the table into three parts according to the aggregate of the two measures: the top three countries have an aggregate score below 10; the middle six countries have an aggregate score between 10 and 12; and the top eight countries have an aggregate score above 12. As Paul notes, these figures suggest much greater support for an *inverse* correlation between religiosity and societal success than for a *direct* correlation between religiosity and societal success. But, if atheism—and, more generally, irreligiosity—were systematically linked with immorality, then these national correlations would be immensely puzzling: how could the aggregate moral conditions created by morally superior people fail to be superior to—and, perhaps even be inferior to—the aggregate moral conditions created by morally inferior people?

Of course, as Paul himself points out, there are limitations on his analysis. We might be able to make better measures of religiosity and societal success that take more factors into account. Perhaps we might be able to find plausible ways to weight the various factors in the two measures. There may well be serious questions about the reliability of some of the data upon which his calculations are based. And so on. Nonetheless, it does seem that currently available cross-national data about societal success challenges the stereotype that atheists are immoral: it seems implausible that societal success scores that reflect the morality of populations would be *higher* for nations that have significantly greater percentages of intrinsically immoral people.

Table 4.1 Religiosity versus societal success

Country	Religiosity	Societal success
United States	0.9	2.9
Ireland	2.3	5.3
Italy	3.9	5.6
Australia	6.1	4.8
Austria	4.9	5.4
Spain	5.4	5.0
Switzerland	5.2	5.7
Canada	5.5	6.2
New Zealand	5.9	5.0
Holland	6.6	6.9
England	7.6	6.2
Germany	8.3	5.7
France	8.5	5.8
Norway	7.5	8.0
Japan	9.2	6.0
Denmark	8.8	7.3
Sweden	9.3	7.1

4.2.4 NIHILISM AND SCEPTICISM

One very pervasive stereotype of atheists is that there are nihilistic sceptics: they do not believe in anything and they do not value anything. This stereotype is belied by a vast amount of social scientific research. As Zuckerman (2009a) reports, there is extensive evidence that shows that, in comparison with their religious peers in the United States, the 'nones' (i.e. those who have no religion) are *less* nationalistic, ethnocentric, racist, sexist, homophobic, closed-minded and authoritarian, *more* supportive of gender equality, women's rights, abortion rights, gay rights, decriminalisation of recreational drugs, stem cell research and doctor-assisted suicide, *less* supportive of torture, draconian sentencing, foreign military intervention and the death penalty, and *more* inclined to liberal, progressive, left-wing politics. Far from suggesting that the 'nones' are nihilistic sceptics, the evidence indicates that, on average, the 'nones' merely have *different* values and beliefs from those held by their religious peers. Of course, atheists are a small minority even among the 'nones'; nonetheless, merely given Zuckerman's findings, it would strain credulity to suppose that, among the 'nones', atheists are uniquely distinguished by their lack of beliefs and values. And, in any case, there is a fast-growing body of recently conducted research that bears out the conclusion that atheists are no more nihilistically sceptical then are devout religious believers.

In order to probe the stereotype that atheists are nihilistic sceptics—non-conformist, cynical, sceptical, joyless, lacking awe and with no basis for morality—Caldwell-Harris et al. (2017) studied a cohort of atheists, Christians and Buddhists using five scales for psychometric assessment. On the *Spirituality Scale*, participants rated their agreement with each of 23 items on a four-point Likert scale (1 = 'strongly disagree'; 4 = 'strongly agree'), yielding information about search for meaning and purpose, relationship, recognition of holism, and connection to the environment and the cosmos. On the *Magical Ideation Scale*, participants rated their agreement with each of 30 items on a six-point Likert scale, yielding information about schizotypal personality disorder. On the *Friedman Well-Being Scale*, participants rated themselves on a ten-point scale for each of 20 pairs of bipolar adjectives (e.g. 'angry'/'calm') as descriptions of their current emotional state. On the *Self-Compassion Scale*, participants rated their agreement with each of 26 items on a four-point Likert scale, yielding information about self-kindness, self-judgment, common humanity, isolation, mindfulness, and over-identification. On the *Interpersonal Reactivity Index*, participants rated their agreement with each of 28 items on a four-point Likert scale, yielding information about perspective taking, empathic concern, emotionality, and selfless concern for the welfare of others. Further, participants were surveyed about their religious beliefs, frequency of church attendance, frequency of prayer/meditation, changes in religion between childhood maturity, reasons for any changes in religion, and the value/utility of their religious beliefs in their lives. Finally, the atheists in the cohort were given some free-response questions:

(a) Who or what influences your moral decisions?
(b) How did you come to believe that God does not exist?
(c) How old were you when you came to this belief?
(d) Has your view changed over the years?
(e) Are/Were one or both of your parents atheists?
(f) Have you ever felt wonderment or felt as if you were part of something greater than yourself?
(g) If so, what provoked these feelings?
(h) What do you attribute them to?

On analysis of the collected data, Caldwell-Harris et al. found no differences between atheists, Buddhists, and Christians for: finding meaning in life experiences, having a sense of purpose, striving to correct excess in lifestyle practices, being happy with who they have become, endorsing respect for nature, endorsing living in harmony with nature, and sometimes feeling at one with the universe; and nor did they find any differences on measures of sociality, joviality, emotional stability, happiness, compassion, and empathic concern. Perhaps the most significant difference between the atheists and the combined Buddhists and Christians was over statements that employed terms like 'spirit', 'spiritual', and 'sacred'. However, while atheists scored lower on these statements, there was no difference in the scores for similar statements that did not contain these particular trigger terms. (Among the free responses for atheists, perhaps the most notable results are that 85 per cent of the atheists said that their moral decisions were motivated by their moral principles, and that 73 per cent of those who had been religious earlier in life gave up their religious beliefs for intellectual reasons.)

The results of Caldwell-Harris et al. (2017) provide support for the view that atheists are relatively intellectual, freethinking and non-conformist; to this extent, there may be something in popular stereotypes. However, their results contradict the view that atheist are relatively cynical, joyless, lacking in awe, lacking in a sense of purpose, and lacking in a foundation for moral decision-making; on all of these counts, popular stereotypes seem to be manifestations of nothing more than untutored prejudice.

Smith (2011) provides an interesting study of identity formation in self-avowed atheists in the United States based on forty in-depth interviews of atheists in Colorado. Given that thirty-five of those interviewed had upbringings somewhere between 'religious' and 'extremely religious', the account that Smith develops of the construction of atheist identity in the United States involves a trajectory from (a) accepting theism, to (b) questioning theism, to (c) rejecting theism, to (d) 'coming out' atheist. In Smith's cohort, most began to experience serious doubts about the existence of God when they first left home to attend college. An initial 'general dissatisfaction' with their previous religious beliefs developed into more particular concerns about the credibility of the Bible, the hypocritical behaviour of some religious believers, the foundation of morality in integrity, autonomy and social benefit, and the superiority of scientific and secular explanation across a wide range of subject matters. As they moved from questioning theism to rejecting theism, these concerns became beliefs and values integrated into self-conceptions on which theists are viewed as 'other': less well-educated, less knowledgeable about science, less rational, more prone to form beliefs in the absence of adequate supporting evidence, less sophisticated, motivated by a crude carrot-and-stick morality, more prone to see violence as a proper way to resolve disagreement, and so on. Finally, when an identity as 'atheist' was explicitly claimed and validated in meaningful social interaction, participants declared themselves to have freely embraced their real or true selves, having fully taken on beliefs and values that markedly distinguish them from their religious compatriots. As Smith (2011: 234) says:

> These atheists found an effective, institutionally grounded, meaning structure which provided a framework for self-understanding; a secular worldview within which they could situate themselves and find a sense of direction, purpose, and legitimation of their viewpoint by appealing to science, reason, and a secular value system.

One interesting feature of Smith's account is that it suggests that the members of her cohort developed questionable stereotypes of their religious compatriots in the course of making their journey from belief to unbelief. It would be interesting to have similar studies of atheists who have never been theists, and, in particular, atheists whose ancestors, going back several generations, were also atheists. Moreover, it would be interesting to have similar studies from more secular countries. It is conceivable that, in some places, at some times, atheism is much less important for identity than it is for the cohort that Smith studied. Be this as it may, it is clear that Smith's study strongly supports the claim that atheists are not nihilistic sceptics: the atheists in her study all developed robust atheistic beliefs and values as they made their journeys from theism to atheism.

4.2.5 UNHAPPINESS AND UNHEALTHINESS

A cluster of stereotypes allege comparatively low levels of physical health, mental health, emotional stability, sexual orthodoxy, altruism and general happiness among atheists.

There is a substantial, longstanding, social scientific literature that claims connections between religiosity/spirituality and various dimensions of physical health. Levin and Vanderpool (1991), reviewing literature from the previous hundred years, declare strong support for the claim that religious involvement exercises a 'protective role' in connection with cardiovascular disease, gastrointestinal disease, uterine cancer, other cancers, mortality, and hypertension. A decade later, Powell, Shahabi, and Thoresen (2003) find, in the then extant literature, persuasive evidence that church attendance protects against death, some evidence that religiosity/spirituality protects against cardiovascular disease, some evidence that being prayed for improves physical recovery from acute illness, some evidence that religiosity/spirituality impedes recovery from acute illness, and insufficient or null evidence that religiosity/spirituality protects against cancer mortality or disability, slows the progress of cancer, promotes longer lives, or protects against death. Very recently, Hayward et al. (2016) find that religious affiliates do not differ overall from atheists and agnostics on physical health outcomes, although atheists and agnostics do better on some individual measures, including obesity, number of chronic conditions, and physical limitations.

There is also a substantial, longstanding, social scientific literature that claims connections between religion/spirituality and various dimensions of mental health and social well-being. For example, Hayward et al. (2016) used a battery of scales to collect reports about positive affect, happiness, life satisfaction, self-esteem, depression, general anxiety, death anxiety, gratitude, optimism, meaning in life, humility, compassion, forgiveness of others, self-forgiveness, emotional support received, emotional support provided, sense of loneliness, cigarette consumption, alcohol consumption, illicit drug use and exercise. They found, among other things, that: (a) those with religious affiliation or no preference reported higher mean happiness, self-esteem, and optimism, and lower mean anxiety than atheists and agnostics; (b) those with religious affiliation or no preference reported lower mean depression than agnostics; and (c) those with religious affiliation reported higher mean levels of compassion, gratitude, giving and receiving emotional support, and sense of meaning of life, and lower levels of alcohol and cigarette consumption, than any of the other three categories, and lower levels of mean loneliness than atheists.

One feature of almost all of the literature on religiosity and health is its failure to consider strength of conviction—and, more generally, robustness of commitment in beliefs and values—among the non-religious. For example, Hayward et al. measure religiosity using a single 'Showcard' response for religious affiliation: there is no God; not sure if there is a God; no religious preference; and more than eighty further 'religious preferences'. Even if it is true that there are physical and mental health advantages for those who claim religious affiliation in comparison with those who claim no religious affiliation, and in comparison with those who claim to be atheists and agnostics, given the measure that Hayward et al. use for determining membership in those classes, it is an open question whether there is any difference in the physical and mental health profiles of those who have robust religious beliefs and values and those who have robust secular beliefs and values.

The idea that there is a need for more fine-grained examination of the class of atheists and agnostics is not new. For example, Ross (1990) found that there is a curvilinear effect of religious belief on psychological distress: similarly low levels of psychological distress are found among those with strong religious beliefs and those with strong secular beliefs. In her study, *psychological well-being* was measured by the number of times in the preceding year that participants had (a) wondered if anything is worthwhile, (b) been in low spirits, (c) had trouble sleeping, (d) had periods when they could not get going, (e) felt that things never turn out right, (f) had trouble remembering things, (g) felt irritable, and (h) felt restless; *religious preference* was measured by a choice from among Protestant, Catholic, Jewish, other, and no religion; *strength of religious belief* was measured on a scale from '0' ('no religion') to '3' ('strong [religious preference]'); and *content of belief* was measured by two aspects of generalised attributions for success: personal efficacy and trust in God. For her cohort—residents of Chicago and surrounding suburbs—Ross found that Protestants and those with no religion had the lowest distress levels, followed by Catholics, who had significantly higher levels of distress, and then by Jews and others, who had the highest levels of distress. In her view, high levels of commitment and low levels of self-estrangement likely explained the low levels of distress in the case of Protestants and those with no religion.

Much more recently, Paterson and Francis (2017) found—contrary to their expectation that higher levels of religiosity are associated with greater psychological well-being and lower levels of depression, anxiety and stress—that participants who reported strongly atheistic beliefs ('I am certain that there is no God') had the greatest perceived well-being and the lowest reported levels of depression, anxiety and stress. Paterson and Francis (2017: 441) write:

> A trend which may be relevant to our findings, and is being supported in much of the recent literature, is a curvilinear relationship between strength of beliefs and psychological well-being. There is a growing body of evidence to suggest that it is not the content of beliefs, but the clarity and stability of beliefs which is associated with benefits for mental health.

Given the recent trend reported by Paterson and Francis (2017)—and given the apparent neglect of earlier studies, such as Ross (1990), that identify the curvilinear relationship in question—that is, at the very least, good reason to support the increasing number of calls for studies that pay attention to strength of beliefs and values among those who have no religion. See, for example,

Hwang et al. (2011), who emphasise the point that, while many social scientific studies have included samples of those classified as 'low spirituality' or 'none', there is an enormous heterogeneity in these groups that remains to be properly investigated.

The social scientific literature on religiosity and altruism is very interesting. Decety et al. (2015) claim that a study of 1170 Canadian, Chinese, Jordanian, South African, Turkish, and American children aged between five and twelve shows that, across all countries, while (a) parents in religious households reported greater expression of empathy and concern for justice in everyday life in their children than parents in non-religious households reported their children, (b) higher religiosity in children was strongly correlated with lower levels of altruism and higher levels of punitive tendencies. However, Shariff et al. (2016) claim that, after correction for an error in the analysis of Decety et al., the data collected by Decety et al. suggest only that children in highly religious households are only slightly less generous than children from moderately religious households. Nonetheless, there is a significant body of literature that finds 'altruistic hypocrisy' in doctrinally orthodox religious believers. For example, Ji et al. (2006), in a study of 16,000 adolescent students in US and Canadian schools affiliated with a particular conservative evangelical Protestant Church, find that students with higher levels of intrinsic religiosity and doctrinal orthodoxy were less likely to help others and volunteer for the community than those with lower levels of intrinsic religiosity and doctrinal orthodoxy, *even though* those students with higher levels of intrinsic religiosity and doctrinal orthodoxy were much more likely than students with lower levels of intrinsic religiosity and doctrinal orthodoxy to say that altruistic action was very important to them. Similarly, Hustinx et al. (2015), drawing on data from a 1990 study of forty countries, find that the more that people emphasise the importance of God in their lives, the less they are motivated to volunteer, whether for altruistic or self-interested reasons. While this literature does not support any firm conclusions about the relative generosity of those who have robust secular beliefs and values, it would be curious if future research were to confirm that those with robust secular beliefs and values are less altruistic than those with robust religious beliefs and values. (Perhaps it is worth noting that significant confounds arise here because (a) patterns of individual altruism vary robustly with wider political and social organisation, and (b) it is not clear whether contributions to organisations that manifestly advance your *own* interests are properly considered to be altruistic.)

As Zuckerman (2009a) reports, there is a range of studies that show that 'nones' report broadly similar sexual behaviour to religious people, albeit with some exceptions: based on reported data, 'nones' are *somewhat* more likely to have a large number of different lifetime sex partners, engage in oral and anal sex, have extra-marital affairs, engage in pre-marital sex, have less guilt about sexual activities, and watch more pornographic movies. However, interestingly, Edelman (2009), in a study of payment for on-line pornography, finds that more secular US states have lower rates of consumption of on-line pornography than more religious US states; and Rosenbaum (2009) finds that teenagers who take 'virginity pledges' are no less likely to engage in pre-marital sex than teenagers who do not pledge, but are much less likely to protect themselves from pregnancy and disease when they do. Setting aside any worries about possible discrepancies between what people say they do and what they actually do, it is worth emphasising that the differences reported above are typically quite small: for example, in a study by Michael et al. (1995), 84 per cent of 'nones', 83 per cent of Jews, 93 per cent of 'conservative Protestants', 92 per cent of 'mainline Protestants', and 91 per cent of Catholics report having fewer than twenty lifetime sex partners. Of course, as in much of the preceding discussion, we should be careful about extrapolating from data about 'nones' to conclusions about atheists: here, as elsewhere, we simply do not have reliable data about those with robust secular beliefs and values.

4.2.6 CONCLUDING REMARKS

There is ample social scientific evidence of negative stereotyping of atheists: it is widely believed, sometimes even by atheists themselves, that atheists are less trustworthy, more prone to criminality, less moral, more prone to nihilism and scepticism, less healthy, less happy, less generous and more prone to violation of sexual taboos than religious people. However, there is also ample social scientific evidence that calls much of this negative stereotyping into question: in many cases, the social scientific evidence suggests that the popular stereotypes are merely manifestations of anti-atheistic prejudice. And, in those cases where we do not have sufficient social scientific evidence to make definitive judgments about popular negative stereotypes of atheists, we do well to (a) reflect on the fact that many other popular negative stereotypes of atheists have been defeated by social scientific evidence; and (b) step back from espousing the remaining popular negative stereotypes of atheists while we await the collection and analysis of further relevant evidence.

4.3 PROFILING ATHEISTS

There are many sources of demographic data about, and psychological profiles of, 'atheists'. Keysar (2007) analyses data from the 2001 American Religious Identification Survey, which uniformly sampled 50,281 respondents. The 2001 ARIS data suggest that, in 2001, in the US, there were 900,000 atheists in a total adult population of 207,983,000. Kosmin and Keysar (2009) analyse data from the 2008 American Religious Identification Survey, which uniformly sampled 54, 461 respondents, The 2008 ARIS data suggest that, in 2008, in the US, there were 1,621,000 atheists in a total adult population of 228,182,000. The data show that the percentage of atheists in the population grew considerably between 2001 and 2008. Because Kosmin and Keysar (2009) reports information about 'nones' rather than information about atheists, I shall now consider the 2001 ARIS data.

According to the ARIS data, in the US, in 2001, atheists were predominantly young (Table 4.2). They were also predominantly male (70 per cent of atheists, but only 48 per cent of the total population, were male). They were relatively poorly educated: 68 per cent were not (yet) college graduates, compared with 66 per cent of the total population. They had a distinctive regional distribution (Table 4.3). And they had a distinctive political party preference profile (Table 4.4).

While a significant amount of time has elapsed since the collection of the 2001 ARIS data, other studies confirm that it continues to be the case that US atheists are predominantly young,

Table 4.2 Atheists in the US, 2001, by age bracket

Age bracket	Percentage of atheists	Percentage of total population
18–34	55	32
35–49	24	31
50–64	9	21
65+	11	16

Table 4.3 Atheists in the US, 2001, by region

Region	Percentage of atheists	Percentage of total population
Northeast	27	30
North central	19	32
South	18	30
West	36	7

Table 4.4 Atheists in the US, 2001, by political preference

Party	Percentage of atheists	Percentage of total population
Republican	10	30
Democrat	26	32
Independent	50	30
Don't know/refused to say	11	7

predominantly male, more highly concentrated in the northeast and west, more inclined to vote Independent, and more likely to have not (yet) graduated from college.

Although the 2001 ARIS data show that atheists in the US in 2001 had a lower level of graduation from college than the population at large, there is other evidence that suggests above average levels of education attainment among atheists. For example, Larsen and Witham (1998a) find that just 7 per cent of scientists in the US National Academy of Science believe in God;

Ecklund and Scheitle (2007) find that no more than 30 per cent of social scientists and natural scientists in elite US universities believe in God with some degree of conviction at least some of the time; Kohul et al. (2009) find that no more than 51 per cent of members of the American Association of the Advancement of Science believe in God with some degree of conviction at least some of the time; and Gross and Simmons (2009) find that 75 per cent of academics from a broad range of higher education institutions—elite doctoral granting universities, non-elite four-year state schools, small liberal arts colleges, and community colleges—believe in God with some degree of conviction at least some of the time.

Moreover, Kanazawa (2010) finds that there is a negative correlation between intelligence and religious belief in the US (Table 4.5), and Lynn et al. (2009) find that this negative correlation between intelligence and religious belief is seen in data about intelligence and religious belief collected in 137 countries. Of course, none of the results that I have cited here are specifically about atheists; rather, some concern those who lack belief in God, and others concern 'nones'. Since it is possible that there might be a bimodal distribution of intelligence for atheists, we need more data before we can confidently assert that there is a positive correlation between intelligence and atheism.

There is a wide social scientific literature on personality profiling of atheists. Some claim that atheists tend to be 'analytic' rather than 'intuitive' or 'empathetic' or inclined to take 'an emotional perspective'; some find a correlation between atheism and autism. Some claim that atheists tend to be 'non-conformist', 'individual', 'systematic', 'pragmatic', 'open to new experience', possessed of a 'strong internal locus of control', inclined to find meaning in the

Table 4.5 Religiosity and mean IQ, US, 2010

Category	Mean IQ
Not religious at all	103.09
Slightly religious	99.34
Moderately religious	98.28
Very religious	97.14

here and now, and committed to social justice, inclusive altruism and environmentalism. It is unclear to me how much of this profiling has robust foundation in empirical data and how much of it simply reflects less negative stereotypes of atheists than those that I discussed in the previous section of this chapter.

5

COMMON COMPLAINTS

There are many complaints that have been made about atheists, and many objections that have been raised against atheism. In this chapter, we shall examine a range of these complaints and objections: that atheists are *fundamentalists*; that atheists are *political ideologues*; that atheists *hate God*; that atheism is *just another religion*; that atheists are *anti-religion*; that atheists are *immoral*; that atheists are *ignorant*; that atheists are *horrible*; that atheism is *unliveable*; and that atheism is *irrational*. There is a more extended discussion, along similar lines, in Blackford and Schuklenk (2013).

5.1 *ATHEISTS ARE FUNDAMENTALISTS*

In 1910, the General Assembly of the Presbyterian Church affirmed the following list of tenets identified by the Niagara Bible Conference:

(a) the infallibility of scripture;
(b) the virgin birth of Jesus;
(c) the atonement of our sins by the death of Christ;
(d) the bodily resurrection of Jesus; and
(e) the historical reality of the miracles of Jesus.

Those who subsequently rallied around these five fundamental tenets became known as 'fundamentalists'. Over time, 'fundamentalism' has taken on more general meanings: either (1) dogmatic attachment to an established set of commitments; or (2) scriptural literalism *combined with* marking of in group / out group distinctions by appeals to ideals of purity and conservative yearnings for past glories that have become lost to more recent generations. However, since atheism is just the belief that there are no gods, and since atheism certainly does not require dogmatic attachment, it is clear that atheists are not fundamentalists in the former sense; and because there are no atheist scriptures and there is no shared atheistic emphasis on purity and the maintenance of in group / out group distinctions, atheists are also not fundamentalists in the latter sense.

It is more charitable to suppose that those who claim that atheists are fundamentalists have something else in mind: perhaps that atheists are *dogmatists*, or that atheists are *certain* that there are no gods, or that atheists think that they *know* that there are no gods, or that atheists think that they have *proofs* that there are no gods. But, as we noted in §2.5, while it is true that some atheists are dogmatists, and some atheists are certain that there are no gods, and some atheists claim to know that there are no gods, and some atheists claim to have proofs that there are no gods, there is nothing in atheism that requires dogmatism, or certainty, or claims to proof, or claims to knowledge, and there are many atheists who are not dogmatists, not certain, and not claimants to proof and knowledge.

Roberts (2014) reports a conversation with an atheist:

> I stopped. I wanted to ask what he thought about science and spirituality. ... I wanted to, but I didn't because I realised he didn't want to engage with the questions; he already knew the answers. He wasn't interested in a discussion. That's when I got it. I was talking to a fundamentalist.

Maybe he did get it; maybe he was talking to someone with mere dogmatic certainty. But there are other possibilities. Perhaps his interlocutor was not interested in what he judged—rightly or wrongly—would be yet another unproductive discussion that benefitted none of the participating parties. Perhaps, more narrowly, his interlocutor was simply not interested in pursuing the envisioned conversation *then* and *there*. When religious hawkers knock on weekends, I greet them with 'Not interested' and close the door. Strictly speaking, of course, I am deeply interested: most of my working week is given over to discussion of philosophy of religion. But there is a time and a place for everything.

5.2 *ATHEISTS ARE POLITICAL IDEOLOGUES*

Many of the world's atheists are Marxists. Marxism is a family of explicitly atheistic political ideologies. However, there is a sense in which it is a mistake to suppose that opposition to religious belief is central to Marxist thought. At the dawn of the twentieth century, Lenin (1905/1954: 10–12) wrote:

> We shall now probably have to follow the advice Engels once gave to the German Socialists: to translate and widely disseminate the literature of the eighteenth-century French enlighteners and atheists. ... But ... it would be stupid to think that ... religious prejudices could be dispelled by purely propaganda methods. ... We do not and should not prohibit proletarians who still retain vestiges of their old prejudices from associating themselves with our Party. ... The revolutionary proletariat will succeed in making religion a really private affair so far as the state is concerned.

In the immediate aftermath of the Russian revolution, Bukharin and Preobrazhensky (1920/1969: §92), faithfully echoed the much earlier claims of Marx and Engels:

> The transition from socialism to communism, the transition from the society which makes an end of capitalism to the society which is completely freed from all traces of class division and class struggle, will bring about the natural death of all religion and superstition.

While Lenin—and Bukharin and Preobrazhensky—were implacably opposed to any involvement of religion in the running of the state, they believed (as Lenin says) that 'everyone must be absolutely free to profess any religion he pleases'. Of course, they also believed—as something resembling an article of faith—that religion would, like the state itself, 'wither away' in the fullness of time. Yet, so long as the state remained in existence, so, too, would 'ecclesiastical and religious societies'; but only as 'free associations of like-minded entities' that were entirely financially and organisationally independent of the state and that did not, in any way, threaten to impede the flowering of the 'dictatorship of the proletariat'. If we look for fundamental explanation of the atrocities committed by communist states, we find it not in those states' commitments to atheism, but rather in their commitment to doing whatever it takes to make it the case that 'workers control the means of production'.

It is sometimes said that Nazis were atheists. This claim is probably false. There is broad scholarly consensus that the core of Nazism is racist social Darwinian eugenics, and, in particular, virulent anti-Semitism. But there is no similar consensus when it comes to the religious commitments of Nazis. Some scholars claim that Nazis were committed to a polytheistic völkisch neo-paganism; some hold that the Nazis were deists; some say that the Nazis adopted a sacralisation of blood and nation; and, most recently, Weikart (2016) argues that the Nazis were pantheists. When we examine Hitler's writings and speeches, we can find what looks like support for the attribution of each of these positions to him. (We can also find what looks like support for the claim that Hitler was committed to an idiosyncratic kind of Christianity; but it is clear that Hitler was no friend of the Christian churches, and that he was contemptuous of much mainstream Christian teaching.) However, if Nazis were pantheists, or deists, or committed to a polytheistic völkisch neo-paganism, then Nazis were not atheists; and even if Nazis were merely adoptees of a sacralisation of blood and nation, it is unclear whether this brought with it some kind of commitment to the existence of gods. It is perhaps reasonable to conjecture that some Nazis were deists, and some Nazis were pantheists, and some Nazis were neo-pagan polytheists, and some Nazis were sacralisers of blood and nation, and some Nazis were at least nominally Christian, and some Nazis fell into more than one of these categories. But, if that is the case, then it would be drawing a very long bow to suggest that atheism played any significant role in the atrocities that were committed by Nazis.

There is social scientific data about atheism and political affiliation; and, though *we* must treat this data with some care, there is also social scientific data about lack of religious affiliation and political affiliation, and about atheism and agnosticism and political affiliation. According to Lipka (2016), a 2015 US survey shows that 15 per cent of atheists are Republicans, 69 per cent are

Democrats, and the remaining 17 per cent are Independents, or would not say, or the like. According to Lugo (2012), in the US, 13 per cent of atheists and agnostics are conservatives, 32 per cent are moderates, 51 per cent are liberals, and the remaining 4 per cent were 'other'. In the US, there is a fairly strong correlation between atheism and 'left-leaning', 'liberal' politics; but, nonetheless, there are significant numbers of atheists who are 'right-leaning' and 'conservative' in their politics. Indeed, Lugo et al. (2012) provide a breakdown for atheists and agnostics according to their party allegiance and their broader political leanings (Table 5.1).

These data show that the majority of Republican or Republican-leaning atheists are conservative or moderate, while the majority of Democrat or Democrat-leaning atheists are liberal. This data is highly problematic for anyone who wants to claim that atheists are political ideologues: given that atheists have significant representation right across the political spectrum, it seems that anyone who holds that atheists are political ideologues will end up committed to the claim that we are all political ideologues. But, if we are all political ideologues, then it is no differential criticism of any group of us that *they* are political ideologues.

5.3 *ATHEISTS HATE GODS*

On the face of it, the claim that atheists hate gods—or some gods, or God—seems clearly mistaken. As Schweizer (2011: 7) says in his study of examples of god-hating in literary fiction, 'No atheist, no matter how passionate, can really hate a divinity they consider to be non-existent in the first place.'

Table 5.1 Atheism and political affiliation in the US, 2012

	Conservative	*Moderate*	*Liberal*	*Don't know*
Republican or Republican-leaning	42	43	13	2
Non-aligned	11	43	25	21
Democrat or Democrat-leaning	3	23	73	1

Some might point to social scientific studies that appear to lend support to the claim that some atheists hate gods. For example, Exline et al. (2011: 146) conducted a series of studies which suggest 'that anger toward God is a relevant concept for some atheists'. However, as Exline et al. themselves note, in one of their studies, they asked atheist participants to recall a negative incident about which they reasoned that harm would not have ensued if God existed and to rate their emotions and attributions regarding God just after the incident; and, in another study, atheist participants were asked to recall a negative incident and to rate what their current emotions and attributions regarding God would be if it were the case that God exists. Whereas Exline et al. bemoan 'a lack of precision in how we assessed anger toward God among [atheists]', we might rather suggest that neither of their studies is designed to measure anger toward God in atheists. Instead, it seems, we are measuring something like *hypothetical* anger: 'How would you feel towards God if you were an out-of-town Midianite who returned home some weeks after the events described in Numbers 31?'

One complicating factor here is that we *may* suppose that we can experience real emotions in connection with what we know are fictional subject matters. Some philosophers think that, when we are absorbed in horror movies, we experience real fear, revulsion, relief, and so forth. However, this is tricky: there is some sense in which, even at the time, we know that the emotions that we feel when we are absorbed in stories are simulacra. In the movies, we may cover our eyes; but, in reality, we fight or flee. Thus, even if we experience 'real' fear when we are watching Godzilla on the big screen, it is not clear that it is exactly right to say that we are afraid of Godzilla. Someone who alerts the army and starts fortifying their home might genuinely be afraid of Godzilla; but they would also be sadly out of touch with reality. So: atheists who read Biblical narratives may genuinely be moved to anger by accounts of divine actions; but, even if so, it does not seem exactly right to say that those atheists are angry with God.

I suspect that common narratives that claim that atheists hate God—or that atheists rebel against God's authority, or that atheists are simply in denial about their true beliefs—are founded in eighteenth century European denigration of atheists. In Europe, during the eighteenth century, it was widely insisted that it is impossible for there to be 'theoretical', or 'speculative', or 'contemplative' atheists whose atheism is 'reasoned', or 'serious', or 'the result of thought'. Instead, according to those running this line, there can only be what Berman (1988) calls 'unthinking' atheism, founded in 'pride', or 'affectation', or 'indolence', or 'wantonness of heart', or 'stupidity', or 'ignorance', or 'immorality', or the like. Among 'unthinking' atheists, there can be those who profess to be theists, but whose immoral actions confirm that they do not really believe in God: these were often called 'practical' atheists. Moreover, among 'unthinking' atheists who do not profess to be theists, there can be those whose atheism is not the product of intellectual shortcomings: 'stupidity', 'ignorance', 'indolence', and the rest. Given that these 'unthinking' atheists cannot be 'theoretical' atheists, the scheme of classification forces the conclusion that they hate God—or rebel against God—because of their pride, or affectation, or wantonness of heart, or immorality, or the like. For example, we read, in an essay in the *London Magazine* in 1734:

A contemplative atheist is what I think impossible; most who would be thought atheists are so out of indolence, because they will not give themselves time to reason, to find if they are so or not: It is rather from wantonness of their heart than the result of their thoughts.

(Cited in Berman 1988: 1)

And, in the *Encyclopedia Britannica* in 1771 we find:

Many people, both ancient and modern, have pretended to atheism, or have been reckoned atheists by the world; but it is justly questioned whether any man seriously adopted such a principle. These pretensions, therefore, must be founded on pride and affectation.

(Cited in Berman 1988: 1)

The obvious thing to say in response to this line of thought is that it is patently an expression of gross unfounded prejudice. In recent times, some atheists (e.g. Rey 2007)—have turned the tables, insisting that no one with standard Anglo-European high school education is really a theist: in effect, the claim is that it is impossible for there to be 'theoretical', or 'speculative', or 'contemplative' theists whose theism is 'reasoned', or 'serious', or 'the result of thought'. While an atheist's inner child may squeal with approval at this historical equalisation, the sober truth is that this view is no more edifying than the counterpart view that has been adopted by many generations of theists. It is a simple fact that there are 'theoretical', or 'speculative', or 'contemplative' atheists whose atheism is 'reasoned', or 'serious', or 'the result of thought', and it is foolish to insist that these atheists *hate* God in any sense that is incompatible with taking that attitude towards mere creatures of fiction.

5.4 ATHEISM IS JUST ANOTHER RELIGION

There are many US religious internet warriors who insist that atheism is a religion. Often enough, they say that their view is supported by decisions taken by US Federal Courts. The First Amendment to the US Constitution tells us that:

> Congress shall make no law respecting an establishment of religion or prohibiting the free exercise thereof; or abridging the freedom of speech, or of the press; or the right of the people peaceably to assemble and to petition the Government for a redress of grievances.

But, in order to suppose that the First Amendment provides certain kinds of legal rights, freedoms and protections for atheists, are we not thereby required to suppose that atheism is a religion?

Not at all. The legal interpretation of the religion clauses in the First Amendment is governed by historical precedent; the US Supreme Court has long insisted that the religion clauses forbid both discrimination in favour of one religion over others and discrimination in favour of religion against irreligion. When it is said—as it sometimes is—that, for US legal purposes, atheism is a religion, this is just a shorthand way of saying that legal precedent has established that the First Amendment provides rights, freedoms, and protections for atheists. This shorthand does not establish *any* other sense in which it is correct to say that atheism is a religion.

Is there some other sense in which atheism is a religion? Clearly, we can say that comprehensive atheistic worldviews, and comprehensive theistic worldviews, and comprehensive religious worldviews, and comprehensive irreligious worldviews address a common set of questions: all comprehensive worldviews make claims about gods, afterlives, morality, ultimate origins, and so forth. If there were nothing more to religion than worldview, then the difference between atheism and religion would merely be that, while atheism is characterised by a single, simple claim—there are no gods—any particular religion is characterised by a multitude of complex claims. And, in that case, while it would not be quite right to say that atheism is a religion, the difference between atheism and religion would not be particularly dramatic.

But, of course, there is much more to religion than worldview; typically, religion also involves designated behaviours and practices (feasts, funerary rites, initiations, prayers, rituals, sacrifices, sermons, and the like); hierarchies; institutions and organisations; leaders and holy people; moral codes; public service; sacred objects; sacred sites; and sacred texts. While belonging to a religion involves taking on a particular kind of comprehensive worldview, belonging to a religion also requires participation in designated behaviours and practices, membership in particular hierarchies, institutions and organisations, conformity to prescribed moral codes, performing certain kinds of public service, and having appropriate regard for certain sacred objects, sites, and texts. But there are no similar requirements for atheists: being an atheist requires no more than holding the belief that there are no gods. Atheism is distinguished from religion by its *lack of requirements* in connection with designated behaviours and practices, hierarchies, institutions and organisations, leaders and holy people, moral codes, public service, sacred objects, sites, and texts, and the like.

Some claim that atheism is a religion because it is based on faith. The grain of truth in this claim is that adoption of a comprehensive worldview is clearly a matter of judgment: there is no algorithm that certifies that, say, comprehensive atheistic worldviews are the best comprehensive worldviews. But there are many other elements of religious faith—embodied in religious behaviour and religious practice—that need find no echo in the lives of irreligious atheists. Some may continue to claim that atheism is faith-based religion, insisting that atheists worship false gods, have their own prophets and preachers, subscribe to their own orthodoxies, have their own punishments for apostasy, run their own institutions and organisations, and so on. But the simple truth is that atheist organisations—such as Ateistisk Selskab, Ateizm Derneği, Atheist Alliance International, American Atheists, Atheism UK, Atheist Foundation of Australia, and Libres Penseurs Athées—play no role at all in the lives of most atheists.

Even if, contrary to fact, it turns out that atheism is a religion, it is not clear what mileage theists might gain from this outcome. If atheism is a religion, then, surely, theism is one, too. But no significant objection to theism turns on the claim that theism is a religion. So, it seems, appeal to the claim that atheism is a religion can do nothing to advance the credentials of theism or to damage the credentials of atheism.

5.5 ATHEISTS ARE ANTI-RELIGION

Whether atheism is antithetical to religion might be taken to depend upon whether theism is essential to religion. If there are—or even if there can be—atheistic religions, then it is immediately obvious that atheism is not anti-religion. In order to determine whether there are atheistic religions, we need to determine whether there are religions that are committed to the claim that there are no gods. And in order to determine whether there could be atheistic religions, we need to determine whether there could be religions that are committed to the claim that there are no gods. Both of these determinations are difficult.

It is often said that there are atheistic branches of major world religions: Hinduism, Buddhism, Taoism, Jainism, and the like. However, no cases are straightforward: there is always room for dispute about whether certain postulated entities are properly considered to be gods. Moreover, if we start with an actual religious worldview, purge it of anything that could be considered to be a god, and then add to it the claim that there are no gods, there will be room for dispute about whether that worldview could be the worldview of something that is properly taken to be a religion.

While I'm inclined to resolve this matter in a way that allows that there can be—and perhaps even are—atheistic religions, I expect that not everyone will be persuaded. No matter. While the existence of atheistic religions would demonstrate that atheism is not anti-religious, uncertainty about the existence of atheistic religions need not translate into uncertainty about whether atheism is anti-religious. Even if it were true that there cannot be anti-theistic religions, that is no reason to suppose that atheists are anti-religion. As we noted in the previous section, religion involves much more than worldview; there is no obvious reason why atheists must be opposed to the participation of others in religious behaviours, hierarchies, institutions, organisations, practices, and the like. Unless the mere contention that religious worldviews are false is held to suffice to show that atheists are anti-religion, there is ample scope for atheists to be neutral or pro-religion. And, of course, if the contention that a particular religious worldview is false is held to suffice for being anti-that-particular-religion, then proponents of any given religion are anti-all-of-the-other-religions. In this case, atheists do not look *very* different from religious adherents; there are just anti-one-more-religion than religious adherents.

5.6 *ATHEISTS ARE IMMORAL*

There are many ways in which atheists are said, by some, to be immoral: (a) atheists are moral relativists; (b) atheists are selfish; (c) atheists don't give to charity; (d) atheists reject the sanctity of human life; (e) atheists deny that morality depends upon divine fiat; (f) atheists deny that we have immortal souls; (g) atheists are lascivious hedonists; and so on. These complaints divide into two major categories. First, there are complaints about the morals of atheists: there are (uncontroversial) moral *principles* by which atheists fail to abide. Second, there are complaints about atheistic understandings of morality: atheists have mistaken *theories* about morality and related matters.

5.6.1 *MORAL PRINCIPLE*

There is widespread agreement across the planet on fundamental moral principles. In all cultures, at all times, there are proscriptions on killing, maiming, sexually assaulting, stealing, extorting, swindling, defaming, lying, and so forth. Of course, there are variations in the details of these proscriptions. For example, in connection with killing, there is variation concerning who may not be killed, who may not engage in a killing, and so forth. All cultures, at all times, have permitted some killing in self-defence, and some killing to protect kith and kin. Many cultures have permitted state authorised killings for certain kinds of offenses (such as treason). Most cultures, at most times, have permitted their militaries and their police forces to kill in some circumstances. Most cultures, at most times, have permitted killing of non-human animals for a range of commercial, industrial, and recreational purposes. And so on. If we frame it correctly, the fundamental moral principle, on which almost all agree, is that *we ought not to kill but may do so in a range of special circumstances*. Of course, there is disagreement about the extent of the permission to kill: for example, some, but not all, cultures permit voluntary euthanasia and assisted suicide. And there is disagreement about what counts as killing: for example, some, but not all, cultures hold that first-trimester abortion is killing, and those that do not suppose that first-trimester abortion is killing typically allow first-trimester abortion. But these kinds of disagreements do not overturn the obvious truth that there is a universally recognised prohibition on killing that leads us all to agree that we ought not to kill (where, of course, the proviso about special circumstances remains tacitly understood). Moreover, there is nothing special about *killing*: there are similar, universally recognised proscriptions on a whole range of actions, including some for which there are no provisos about special circumstances (e.g. that we ought not to engage in sexual assault). And there is also nothing special about *prohibitions*: there are similar, more or less universally recognised prescriptions for a whole range of actions, with or without provisos about special circumstances (e.g. that we should all have some engagement in helping the less fortunate among us).

Given that there is widespread agreement about fundamental moral principles, it is entirely unsurprising that atheists are party to that agreement. In §4.2.3, we noted that cross-national data about societal success strongly confirms that atheists do no worse than everyone else in conforming to these fundamental moral principles. If, for example, we look at data about killing, we find no reason at all to suppose that atheists are less respectful than others of the norm that we ought not to kill. (And this is true even in cases where it is contested whether there are special circumstance provisos: for example, there is no evidence that atheists present at higher rates for abortion than populations at large.) As we have already had occasion to note, it is a gratuitous calumny to claim that atheists behave less morally than others.

5.6.2 *MORAL THEORY*

Allegations that atheists have mistaken moral theories divide into two groups. Some allege that atheists have mistaken *normative* moral theories: they have mistaken views about what morality *claims*. Other allege that atheists have mistaken meta-ethical theories: they have mistaken views about what morality *is*. Normative ethics and meta-ethics are hotly contested philosophical domains; there is no convergence of expert philosophical opinion in either area. Among the contested theories in these domains, distinctively theistic theories all fall somewhere in the ballpark of *divine command theories*: theories that claim (a) that morality is a special kind of divine fiat, and (b) that the actual content of morality is given by some particular recording of alleged divine decrees. There are various well-known objections to divine command theories—e.g. that the content of morality could not possibly be established by arbitrary divine fiat, and that there is insufficient reason to suppose that any recording of basic moral laws has divine origination—but here I shall focus on the difficulties that arise because of the evident incompleteness of extant recordings of alleged divine decrees.

Existing theistic tabulations of putative divine decrees are mixtures of (a) principles that are universally accepted and (b) principles that are more or less broadly contested. Because the extant recordings contain many principles that are universally accepted—do not kill, do not rape, do not steal, help those in immediate need of help, and so forth—these recordings have a significant broad resonance. However, when it comes to questions of application in cases where provisos about special circumstances must be taken into account, it is often the case that the recorded principles yield no verdict. As we noted in §5.6.1, the provisos are open-ended and contested; unsurprisingly, there are no extant recordings in which relevant provisos are spelled out in clear and complete detail. When it comes to practical moral reasoning, it is very often the case that we need to appeal to further moral considerations in order to reach publicly defensible conclusions. But from whence do these further moral considerations proceed? The only plausible answer that I can see to this question is that we turn to the kinds of consequentialist and/or deontological and/or virtue-theoretic considerations that are identified in philosophical theorising about normative morality.

This is just to say that there is nothing that distinguishes theistic—or atheistic—moral theorising from the broader family of moral theorising. Most moral theorists are consequentialists and/or deontologists and/or virtue theorists. Very roughly: if they are *consequentialists*, they suppose that what we are permitted or required to do depends upon the goodness of the consequences of the possible actions open to us; if they are *deontologists*, they suppose that what we are permitted or required to do depends upon the basic rights and responsibilities that accrue to all persons; and if they are *virtue theorists*, they suppose that we are permitted or required to do depends upon our recognition of what it would be virtuous or vicious for us to do. When we think about questions of application of fundamental moral principles in cases where provisos about special circumstances must be taken into account, we *all* appeal to some mixture of considerations about consequences, rights and obligations, and virtues and vices. However, given that we all accept the same basic moral principles, and that we all appeal to similar considerations when handling provisos about special circumstances, there are simply no grounds for supposing that atheists are distinctively immoral. True enough, there are immoral and amoral atheists; indeed, some of the worst psychopaths in history were atheists. But, as we saw in the case of moral principle, there is nothing in considerations about moral theory that singles out atheists as distinctively deviant cases.

5.7 ATHEISTS ARE IGNORANT

As we saw in §5.3, there is a long tradition of insistence that atheists are thoughtless, stupid and ignorant. On the one hand, atheists work with crude caricatures of religion: they do not understand the subtleties that are grasped by at least some religious believers. And, on the other hand, they are in thrall to rudimentary, hopelessly misbegotten views of the universe and our place within it: materialism, scientism, humanism, nihilism, scepticism, and the like.

In §4.3, we noted that there is a significant body of social scientific research that suggests that the average intelligence of atheists is higher than the average intelligence of populations at large, and significantly higher than the average intelligence of very religious people. That research suggests that we should be hesitant to claim that atheists are thoughtless and stupid. But it is consistent with the claim that atheists are not thoughtless and stupid that they *are* ignorant when it comes to questions about religion.

Lugo (2010) reports that, in a Pew survey of religious knowledge in the US that contained 32 questions about religion, the top-scoring group—with an average of 20.9 correct answers—was atheists and agnostics. Jews averaged 20.5; Mormons averaged 20.3; white evangelical Protestants averaged 17.6; white Catholics averaged 16.0; and white mainline Protestants averaged 15.8. While the survey was not large enough to disaggregate atheists and agnostics, it is reasonable to take the results of this survey as an indication that, at least in the US, on average, atheists actually know significantly more about religion than theists. If atheists are particularly ignorant when it comes to questions about religion, it seems that this can only be a matter of very localised pockets of ignorance.

According to the PhilPapers Survey 2009 (https://philpapers. org/surveys/index.html), professional philosophers are 72.8 per cent atheists and 49.8 per cent naturalists, whereas professional philosophers of religion are 72.3 per cent theists and 57.4 per cent non-naturalists. These figures, which display expected connections between (a) theism and non-naturalism and (b) naturalism and atheism, pose an immediate problem for the view that atheists have hopelessly crude worldviews: professional philosophers, to a greater measure than any other group, devote their time to examining and developing worldviews. If atheistic worldviews really are crude, rudimentary, and hopelessly misbegotten, then it is utterly mysterious why 72.8 per cent of professional philosophers are atheists. Of course, that most professional philosophers are atheists does not provide much—if any—reason for thinking that atheism is true; but if, say, naturalism is false, it is implausible to suppose that those naturalistic professional philosophers have made some crude, rudimentary and hopeless misbegotten error in their adoption of naturalism.

One common complaint about atheists is that they do not understand the attraction of religious faith because they are outsiders to religious worldviews: atheists are unable to appreciate from the inside what it is like to be a religious believer. While it might be suggested that this complaint underestimates the powers of the imagination, it is more straightforward to point to the fact— adverted to in the discussion of Smith (2011) in §4.2.4—that many atheists do not give up their prior theism until well into their adult lives. Since there is no significant difference between the worldviews of those atheists who are adult converts from theism and those who are not, and since it can hardly be contested that adult converts from theistic religions know what it is like to be a religious believer, we have strong reason to doubt that there is something it is like to be a religious believer that atheists are unable to appreciate and that leaves atheists with an impoverished understanding of religious faith. (A similar point applies to the complaint that atheists base their criticisms of religion on the behaviour of religious extremists and fail to appreciate the attractions of moderate religion: there is no significant difference between the worldviews of those atheists who are adult converts from moderate religion and those who are not, and yet it can hardly be maintained that adult converts from moderate religion don't know what it is like to be a moderate religious believer.)

5.8 ATHEISTS ARE HORRIBLE

There are many respects in which it has been claimed that atheists are horrible. Atheists are elitists. Atheists are arrogant. Atheists are intolerant. Atheists are hateful. Atheists are vain. Atheists are self-obsessed. Atheists are judgmental. Atheists are disrespectful. Atheists are killjoys. Atheists are humourless. Atheists are out to run society according to their rules. Atheists are out to ban religious people from the public square. Atheists are out to ban teaching about religion from public schools.

Where to start? Some of these claims are bizarre. Even if atheists were out to run society according to their rules, or to ban religious people from the public square, or to ban teaching about religion from public schools, they make up such a small part of the populations of Western democracies that there is no serious prospect that they would succeed. Serious estimates place the percentage of atheists in the US population as low as 0.5 per cent. What magic powers could atheists possess that would make it realistic for them to set out after the goals mentioned above? In any case, it is clear that few—if any—atheists really are out to run society according to their rules, or to ban religious people from the public square, or to ban teaching about religion from public schools. For a start, there is no agreement among atheists about how society ought to be run. As we saw in §5.2, atheists are distributed across the political spectrum, from libertarians to communitarians. Almost all atheists are committed to freedom of speech and freedom of association; almost all atheists want religious people to be included in the public square. Almost all atheists are committed to public education; almost all atheists want the study of world religions to be included in public school curricula.

At best, most of the remaining claims are based on hasty generalisations from small, carefully selected samples. True enough, there are atheists who are elitist, arrogant, intolerant, hateful, vain, self-obsessed, judgmental, disrespectful, killjoys. But there are no social scientific studies that support general attributions of these properties to atheists, or that support the claim that these traits are more common in atheists than they are in the general population. Moreover, it is antecedently highly improbable that general attribution of these properties to atheists fits well with claims—of the kinds discussed in earlier sections of this and the previous chapter—that are supported by social scientific studies. If atheists were elitist, arrogant, intolerant, hateful, vain, self-obsessed, judgmental, disrespectful killjoys, then, by and large, atheists would be unhappy social outcasts. But it is not true, by and large, that atheists are unhappy social outcasts.

That leaves the allegation that atheists are humourless. There are atheist jokes. Here is a modest example. A Jewish atheist enrols his son in what he is told is the best school in town. The school is Catholic. All starts well. Then, one day, his son comes home and says: 'Today, I learned about the Father, the Son, and the Holy Ghost.' The father is furious. 'Steve, listen carefully. This is very important. There is only *one* God … and we do not believe in Him!'

5.9 *ATHEISM IS UNLIVEABLE*

There are various dimensions to the claim that atheism is unliveable. Some say that, for atheists, life is meaningless. Some say that atheists live in fear of death and typically seek divine solace when they are dying. Some say that atheists are constitutionally unable to appreciate art and/or nature and/or a range of other goods that life offers. Some say that atheists are unable to make and sustain principled commitments; many suppose that atheists could never be found in foxholes. And so on.

A natural reply to these kinds of allegations is that it is obvious, in light of the social scientific data that we have been discussing, that atheists lead lives that are not dramatically less flourishing than the lives of everyone else. The predictable response to this reply is that this is only because atheists are self-deceived: by their own lights, they have no grounds on which to claim that their lives are meaningful, that art and nature are worthy objects of appreciation, that death is nothing to be feared, that there are good reasons to take principled stands on a whole range of matters, and that some things are worth fighting for even at the risk of life and liberty.

However, it is a mistake to suppose that atheists cannot have grounds for believing and behaving as they do. Suppose, for example, that atheists say—roughly following Aristotle—that there is a set of rules of thumb that jointly apply to human flourishing: by and large, flourishing people (a) are engaged in worthwhile pursuits and are recognised by other people to be engaged in worthwhile pursuits; (b) belong to communities of flourishing people and have meaningful relationships with people in those communities; (c) have appropriate emotional responses to themselves and others; (d) behave in ways that are both virtuous and morally appropriate; (e) do not have fantastic—wildly irrational—beliefs about themselves and the world to which they belong; (f) do not engage in self-destructive behaviour and excessive risk-taking; and (g) are not overwhelmed by loneliness, stress, low self-esteem, lack of self-control, ignorance, illness and poverty. This *prima facie* plausible account of human flourishing can serve perfectly well as the ground upon which atheists can claim that they lead flourishing lives.

Perhaps it is worth adding that the claim that there are no atheists in foxholes is seriously challenged by the fact that the *frontoviks*—the Soviet riflemen who played a pivotal role in the defeat of the advancing German army during the Second World War—lived, fought, and died in small circular foxholes (Rottman 2007: 46). While not all *frontoviks* were atheists, there is no doubt that a very large percentage of them were. Of course, in countries where atheists are in a very small minority, and in which there are significant costs involved in the disclosure of non-belief to commanding officers, there is likely to be little evidence of atheists in foxholes. But, given even a moment's reflection on the battles of the Cold War (e.g. the Greek Civil War, the First Indochina War, the Malayan War, the Korean War, the Second Indochina War, the Sino-Indian War, the Warsaw Pact Invasion of Czechoslovakia, the Ogaden War, the Third Indochina War, the China-Vietnam War, the Soviet Invasion of Afghanistan, the Invasion of Grenada, and the Romanian Revolution), it is obvious that, in the period of the Cold War alone, there was a vast multitude of atheists in foxholes.

Some may say that the claim that there are no atheists in foxholes is properly understood to be the claim that those who enter foxholes as atheists do not remain atheists for long: in the face of sufficiently serious existential horror, atheism quickly evaporates. But the case of the *frontoviks* is a no less serious challenge to *this* claim: there is no less certainty that a very large percentage of *frontoviks* who emerged from their foxholes were atheists than there is that a large percentage of *frontoviks* were atheists when they entered their foxholes. And, in any case, it is a commonplace that the horrors of the major wars of the twentieth century played a significant role in reducing religious conviction: for many soldiers, foxhole experience led directly to the extinction of prior theistic belief.

Some may say that the claim that there are no atheists in foxholes is properly understood to be the claim that, in the heat of battle, all are theists. While there is evidence that 'non-religious individuals' report stronger implicit religious beliefs when mortality is salient (see Jong and Halberstadt 2016; 2018)—there has not yet been any relevant study of atheists. Moreover, even if it did turn out that atheists have implicit theistic beliefs when mortality is highly salient, it is not clear what implications that would have for the liveability or rationality of atheism. Should we think that the way that some people behave in the immediate aftermath of watching horror movies is good evidence that they *really* believe that there are demons, ghosts, ghouls, and the like?

5.10 *ATHEISM IS IRRATIONAL*

There are various ways in which atheism is said to be irrational. Some say that atheism is rationally self-defeating. Some say that atheism is rationally defeated by logic. Some say that atheism is rationally defeated by evidence. Some say that atheism is rationally defeated by prudence. I shall examine each of these claims in turn.

5.10.1 *SELF DEFEAT*

It seems possible for there to be self-defeating claims. If I say 'I am unable to speak', and what I say is interpreted in a completely flat-footed, literal manner, then it seems that my speaking contradicts the content of what I say. If I say 'I am a solipsist', as a move in a conversation that I am having with someone else, it seems that my making that conversational move contradicts the content of the words that I utter. But, if I utter the words 'there are no gods', no similar considerations apply. Even if I am a god, and I sincerely utter these words, while it will be true that I am mistaken about who I am, it seems that it will not be right to say that my utterance is self-defeating. Compare the case of someone who claims to be 182 cm tall when, in fact, they are only 176 cm tall: what they claim is false, but their making the claim is not, in any sense, self-defeating.

Some may object, against this analysis, that the claim that there are no gods is self-defeating because anyone's saying that there are no gods presupposes that there are gods. This allegation is slippery. On one way of understanding it, what is being claimed is that those who utter the words 'there are no gods' *themselves* suppose that there are gods and that they would not be uttering those words if there were no gods. On a second way of understanding it, what is being claimed is that, while those who utter the words 'there are no gods' do not themselves suppose that there are gods and that they would not be uttering the words if there were no gods, nonetheless, it is *true* that there are gods and that they would not be uttering the words if there were no gods.

On the first interpretation, the obvious thing to say is that atheists do not themselves suppose that there are gods and that they would not be uttering those words if there were no gods. So, on the first interpretation, it is just a mistake to claim that it is self-defeating for atheists to say that there are no gods. On the contrary, when atheists say that there are no gods, they are giving an entirely unproblematic formulation of the belief that is characteristic of atheists.

On the second interpretation, the obvious thing to say is that the fact that there are *other* people who suppose that there are gods and that they would not be uttering those words if there were no gods provides no reason at all for saying that atheism is self-defeating. Of course, if those who say that there are gods and that they would not be uttering those words if there were no gods are correct, then atheism is false. But, equally, if atheism is true, then those who say that there are gods and that they would not be uttering those words if there were no gods are mistaken. That people disagree about a bunch of claims is typically no grounds at all for claiming that the position of those on one side of the dispute is self-defeating.

So long as we are careful in giving an unambiguous interpretation of claims about presupposition, there is no way that we can show that the claim that there are no gods presupposes the claim that there are gods.

5.10.2 *LOGICAL DEFEAT*

Some claims are logically inconsistent. If I say 'It is raining and it is not raining', and if what I say is interpreted in a completely flat-footed literal manner, then the claim that I have made is logically inconsistent. If we use the symbol '&' for conjunction, and the symbol '~' for negation, and the sentence-letter 'p' for the sentence 'it is raining', then the sentence 'it is raining and it is not raining' is properly represented by the sentence 'p & ~p'. This representation makes it clear that the contradiction in the sentence 'it is raining and it is not raining' is both formal and logical: no matter what sentence is assigned to 'p' in the sentence 'p & ~p', the result will be a contradiction: 'grass is green and grass is not green', 'Trump is president and Trump is not president', and so on.

The sentence 'there are no gods' is plainly not a logical contradiction. We can think of this sentence as having the logical form 'There are Fs'. But some sentences of this form are true—'there are dogs', 'there are stars'—and other sentences of this form are false—'there are unicorns', 'there are mountains of gold'. Logic alone does not always tell us, for particular sentences of this form, whether they are true or false. And, in particular, logic alone does not tell us whether 'there are no gods' is true or false.

When people claim that atheism is logically inconsistent, they typically do not mean that the sentence 'there are no gods' is logically inconsistent. Rather, what they have in mind is that there is a wider set of sentences to which atheists are committed that are jointly formally inconsistent. If, for example, atheists believe both that there are gods and that there are no gods, then atheists have a set of beliefs of the form (there are Fs; there are no Fs), and any set of beliefs of this form is logically inconsistent.

Suppose that atheists are committed to a logically inconsistent set of claims that includes the claim that there are no gods. Let 'G' be the claim that there are gods, so that '~G' is the claim that there are no gods. It is a fundamental result in standard classical logic that a set of sentences $\{p_1, \dots , p_n, \sim G\}$ is logically inconsistent if and only if G is a logical consequence of the set of sentences $\{p_1, \dots , p_n\}$. Said differently: a set of sentences $\{p_1, \dots , p_n, \sim G\}$ is logically inconsistent if and only there is a logical derivation of G from $\{p_1, \dots , p_n\}$.

To illustrate. Let '$\rightarrow$' represent the material conditional: we read '$p \rightarrow q$' as 'if p then q', and suppose that '$p \rightarrow q$' is true exactly if it is not the case that p is true and q is false. The following derivation shows both that $\{p, p \rightarrow G, \sim G\}$ is inconsistent and that G is a logical consequence of $\{p, p \rightarrow G\}$:

1   p premise
2   p→G premise
3   ~G premise
4   G from 1 and 2, by modus ponens
5   G&~G from 3 and 4, by conjunction introduction

The derivation to line 4 shows that G follows from $\{p, p \rightarrow G\}$—given A and if A then B, it follows by logic alone that B—and the derivation to line 5 shows that we can derive an explicit contradiction from $\{p, p \rightarrow G, \sim G\}$.

Suppose that we have a logical derivation of G from a set of claims $\{p_1, \ldots, p_n\}$. What properties must the set of claims $\{p_1, \ldots, p_n\}$ have in order for it to be the case that the logical inconsistency of the set of claims $\{p_1, \ldots, p_n, \sim G\}$ poses a serious logical challenge to atheists? The answer is obvious: it must be that atheists believe the claims $\{p_1, \ldots, p_n\}$. So, in particular, if atheists do not believe all of the claims, then they can meet the alleged logical problem that is presented to them through the derivation of G from $\{p_1, \ldots, p_n\}$ simply by observing that they do not believe all of the claims $\{p_1, \ldots, p_n\}$. Nothing more is required. Of course, the conversation may not end at this point; but, unless there is some subsequent change in the beliefs of the atheist, the derivation in question cannot do anything to cast doubt on the logical consistency of the beliefs of the atheist.

Consider, for example, the following derivation:

1   Whatever began to exist had a cause of its beginning to exist. (Premise)
2   Natural reality began to exist. (Premise)
3   If natural reality has a cause of its beginning to exist then there is at least one god. (Premise)
4   There are no gods. (Premise)
5   Natural reality had a cause of its beginning to exist. (From 1, 2)
6   There is at least one god. (From 3, 5)
7   There are no gods and there is at least one god. (From 4, 6)

This derivation shows that the set of claims {whatever began to exist had a cause of its beginning to exist, natural reality began to exist, if natural reality has a cause of its beginning to exist then there is at least one god, there are no gods} is logically inconsistent.

Does this derivation present a serious logical challenge to atheism? Given our previous discussion, and given that the derivation really does show that the set of claims in question are logically inconsistent, the key question is whether atheists believe 1–3.

I shall assume, without argument, that atheists accept 3: the only things that could be causes of the beginning of the existence of natural reality are gods. But that still leaves 1 and 2. Do atheists accept both of them?

To help us think about this question, it is useful to start by considering a slightly different question. Rather than think about the origin of natural reality, let us consider the origin of causal reality. Since causal reality is the whole causal network, it cannot be that there is a cause of causal reality: such a cause both would and would not belong to causal reality. So it cannot be that it is true both that causal reality began to exist and that whatever began to exist had a cause of its beginning to exist. In order to maintain logical consistency, theists and atheists alike must either accept that causal reality did not begin to exist, or else accept that there are some things that began to exist that do not have causes of their beginning to exist.

Among positions that atheists adopt, one very popular position is that causal reality is natural reality: the entire network of causes is just the entire network of natural causes. Atheists who take this position can say about 'natural reality' versions of 1 and 2 whatever theists say about the 'causal reality' versions of 1 and 2: if theists can say that causal reality did not begin to exist, then atheists can say that natural reality did not begin to exist; and if theists can say that causal reality is a counterexample to the claim that whatever began to exist had a cause of its beginning to exist, then atheists can say that natural reality is a counterexample to the claim that whatever began to exist had a cause of its beginning to exist. But, given all of this, it is obvious that the derivation above presents no serious logical challenge to atheism: consistent atheists simply do not accept 1 and 2, just as consistent theists do not accept the 'causal reality' versions of 1 and 2.

Of course, that this derivation does nothing to impugn the logical consistency of atheism does not entail that there are no other derivations that do impugn the logical consistency of atheism. However, I think that it quite safe to say that no one has ever produced a derivation that does present a logical challenge to atheism: wherever theists have found inconsistent sets of sentences that include the claim that there are no gods, it has always turned out that reflective, thoughtful, informed atheists reject one or more of the other claims in the inconsistent set of sentences. Moreover, while past failure does not guarantee future failure, the null return on massive past investment certainly provides no reason at all to expect future success. At the very least, the challenge here for critics of atheism is clear: find a set of unambiguous, clearly articulated claims, including the claim that there are no gods, that can be shown to satisfy the following two conditions: (a) the set of claims is logically inconsistent; and (b) thoughtful, intelligent, reflective, well-informed atheists accept all of the claims in the set. Good luck.

5.10.3 *EVIDENTIAL DEFEAT*

Some claims run contrary to available evidence. For example, the claim that smoking cigarettes poses no danger to health is defeated by a massive amount of contraindicating evidence. Many theists say that the claim that there are no gods is defeated by a similarly massive amount of contraindicating evidence: that there is something rather than nothing; that our part of natural reality is fine-tuned for our existence; that there are irreducibly complex biological entities; that there are reliable reports of divine intervention in human history; that we are capable of logical, mathematical and statistical reasoning; that we have modal knowledge; that we have moral knowledge; that we are moved by the dictates of conscience; that we are capable of appreciating beauty; that we are (sometimes) conscious; that there are reliable reports of direct experience of the divine; that there are scriptures that record important truths about the divine; that we have a capacity for humour; that we have a capacity for love; and so on (and on). In order to fully assess this claim, we need to examine all—or, at any rate, a sufficiently large amount—of the relevant evidence. This is no small task. In this section, I shall examine just one small part of the relevant evidence—the fact that there is something rather than nothing—and argue that it provides no reason to prefer theism to atheism. (I shall return to consider more of this evidence in §6.9.)

Why is there something rather than nothing? There is a very small range of possible answers to this question. We might suppose that there is something rather than nothing because there *must be* something rather than nothing. Or we might suppose that there is something rather than nothing because there *always has been* something rather than nothing. Or we might suppose that there is *no explanation* of why there is something rather than nothing: it is simply a brute fact that there is something rather than nothing. Or we might suppose that there is something rather than nothing because it is *good* that there is something rather than nothing. Moreover—and this is the key point—it seems that each of these accounts is no less available to atheists than to theists. If theists insist that there is something rather than nothing because there must be gods, then atheists can insist that there is something rather than nothing because there must be natural reality. If theists insist that there is something rather than nothing because there have always been gods, then atheists can insist that there is something rather than nothing because there has always been natural reality. If theists insist that there is no explanation of why there are gods, then atheists can insist that there is no explanation of why there is natural reality. And if theists insist that there is something rather than nothing because it is good that there are gods, then atheists can insist that there is something rather than nothing because it is good that there is natural reality. Insofar as we are focussed only on the question why there is something rather than nothing, there is no reason to think that theism has an explanatory advantage over atheism.

Perhaps it is worth extending this discussion a little bit further. Consider the question of the explanation of the existence of natural reality: why is there natural reality? Those theists who suppose that there are gods who created natural reality may suppose that they have an explanatory advantage here: there is no similar story that atheists can tell about the existence of natural reality. However, while it is true that there is no similar story that atheists can tell, this does nothing to support the claim that theists here have an explanatory advantage. Why not? Look back to the discussion in §5.10.2. The story that atheists tell about natural reality can be just like the story that theists tell about causal reality. If, for example, theists say that causal reality exists because gods must exist, then atheists can say that natural reality exists because it must exist. When we look at the total picture, there is no explanatory advantage that accrues to theists; rather, theists and atheists agree that causal reality exists because something must exist, but disagree about what it is that must exist. The existence of natural reality is not better explained by the suggestion that it is created by gods that must exist than it is by the suggestion that natural reality itself must exist: if all that we are considering is the existence of natural reality, then the introduction of creator gods is a fifth wheel to the explanatory coach.

Although I am not going to try to run through the details in this section, I shall say upfront that I think that all of the relevant evidence is amenable to similar kinds of treatment: when we look closely at the details of explanations of evidence, we see that there is no advantage that accrues to theistic explanations over atheistic explanations. At the very least, the challenge for critics of atheism is clear: show that, on examination of the full range of cases that clearly deserve to be called evidence, there are so many cases in which the evidence strongly favours theism over atheism—and so few cases in which the evidence even weakly favours atheism over theism—that it is plausible to insist that the total evidence favours theism over atheism.

5.10.4 *PRAGMATIC DEFEAT*

So far, we have considered a range of objections to atheism from *theoretical* reason: allegations that atheism is logically self-defeating, that atheistic worldviews are logically inconsistent, and that atheistic worldviews are defeated by contraindicating evidence. Even if all of these objections to atheism from theoretical reason fail, there are some who will wish to insist that there are decisive objections to atheism from *practical* reason. First example: some critics of atheism say that, in order for things to go well for us, we need to believe that, in the end, virtue is rewarded and vice is punished; but, in order to believe that, in the end, virtue is rewarded and vice is punished, we need to believe in gods and afterlives. Second example: some critics of atheism say that, *since*, given that there are gods and afterlives, and given that the gods make it a condition of our having happy afterlives that we believe in them, we do so much better to believe in gods and afterlives, *even now*, in order to give ourselves a shot at having happy afterlives, we do better to believe that there are gods and afterlives.

I think that it is not true that, in order for things to go well for us, we need to believe that, in the end, virtue is rewarded and vice is punished. In fact, I suspect that things are likely to go *worse* for those who think that moral motivation—disposition to choose virtue of vice—can be securely founded only in considerations of divine reward and punishment. But, at the very least, the empirical evidence that we have been discussing provides no support at all for the claim that those who believe in gods and afterlives do better than those who believe that there are no gods and afterlives. Moreover, even if it were true that those who believe in gods and afterlives do better than those who believe that there are no gods and afterlives, that would not provide anyone with an appropriate reason to believe that there are gods and afterlives. That my life would go better if I believed that I am sixth in line to the British throne does not give me any kind of reason to believe that I am sixth in line to the British throne. Why suppose that matters go any differently for the belief that there are gods and afterlives?

It seems right to say that, if there are fairies at the bottom of my garden who provide showers of good fortune, and if it is a condition of those fairies at the bottom of my garden showering me with good fortune that I believe that there are fairies at the bottom of my garden who shower good fortune upon those who believe in them, then I will do better to believe that there are fairies at the bottom of my garden who shower good fortune upon those who believe in them. But it does not seem right to conclude from this that, even now, in order to give myself a shot at a shower of good fortune, I do better to believe that there are fairies at the bottom of my garden who shower good fortune upon those who believe in them. Why not? How is this case any different from the case involving gods and afterlives? If it is not right to *conclude* that, even now, in order to give myself a shot at a shower of good fortune, I do better to believe that there are fairies at the bottom of my garden who shower good fortune upon those who believe in them, how can it be right to *conclude* that, even now, in order to give myself a shot at having a happy afterlife, I do better to believe that there are gods and afterlives?

As in the case of our discussions of logical defeat and evidential defeat, we have barely begun to scratch the surface of discussion of allegations that theism is subject to pragmatic defeat. I think that, when we look closely, we find no cases in which mere practical reason provides adequate grounds for belief in gods. At the very least, the challenge for critics of atheism is clear: find one carefully articulated case in which merely practical considerations (i.e. considerations about how we would like things to be or how things would go best for us) really do give us reason to believe that there are gods.

5.11 *CONCLUDING REMARKS*

In this chapter, we have considered a wide range of criticisms of atheists and atheism. We have considered—and rejected—both the claim that atheists are horrible, immoral, ignorant, anti-religious, god-hating, fundamentalist ideologues and the claim that atheism is an irrational, unliveable religion. Throughout this chapter—as in the previous chapter—we have been at pains to argue that there is very little that distinguishes between atheists and others, and that, where there are differences, those differences are typically on a very small scale. On historical global average, as far as we can tell, atheists are very similar to everyone else in their niceness, morality, knowledgeability, rationality, attachment to ideologies, and so forth.

6

REASONS AND ARGUMENTS

There are various strategies that might be pursued by those arguing for atheism. We begin by explaining the theoretical vocabulary that is used in setting out the range of strategies.

6.1 *BIG PICTURES, DATA AND WORLDVIEWS*

We start with 'theism' and 'atheism' as defined in §2.1. Among the beliefs of atheists, we shall say that *atheistic beliefs* are those beliefs that have some logical or evidential or explanatory relevance to their atheism; and, among the beliefs of theists, we shall say that *theistic beliefs* are those beliefs that have some logical or evidential or explanatory relevance to their theism.

Given that atheistic beliefs are logically consistent, we can consider their non-trivial logical closure; and given that theistic beliefs are logically consistent, we can consider their non-trivial logical closure. (A set of sentences S is *logically closed* if and only if every sentence that is entailed by sentences that belong to S is itself a member of S. Said differently: a set of sentences is logically closed if and only if every logical consequence of members of S is itself a member of S. The *logical closure* of a set of sentences S is the set of sentences that is arrived at by adding sentences that are logical consequences of sentences already in S until there are no more sentences to be added. A set of sentences S has a *non-trivial logical closure* if and only if not every sentence belongs to the logical closure of S. Said differently: A set of sentences has a non-trivial logical closure if and only if S is logically consistent.) I shall call the logical closure of a set of logically consistent atheistic beliefs an *atheistic big picture*; and I shall call the logical closure of a set of theistic beliefs a *theistic big picture*.

Big pictures divide into two parts: that which is common to a range of competing big pictures, which I call *data*, and that which is distinctive of particular big pictures, which I call *worldview*. So, for a given atheistic big picture and theistic big picture, what they agree on is data, and what they disagree on is, respectively, *atheistic worldview* and *theistic worldview*.

6.2 OVERVIEW OF STRATEGIES

With the notions of big picture, data and worldview in hand, we can now proceed to explain various strategies that might be adopted by those arguing for atheism:

(a)   Some argue that atheism—the claim that there are no gods— is a default belief and that there is no reason to give it up.

(b)   Some argue that theism—the claim that there is at least one god—is meaningless, or logically inconsistent, or otherwise deficient in ways that can be exhibited without considering any other relevant claims.

(c)   Some argue that, while theism is not deficient in ways that can be exhibited without considering any other relevant claims, theistic worldviews—and, in particular, best theistic worldviews—are logically inconsistent.

(d)   Some argue that, while best theistic worldviews are logically consistent, best theistic big pictures are logically inconsistent.

(e)   Some argue that, while best theistic big pictures are logically consistent, best theistic big pictures are less theoretically virtuous than best atheistic big pictures.

Before we turn to an examination of each of these kinds of arguments, we need to introduce some elementary theory of argumentation. In particular, we need to be clear that we understand what it takes for an argument to be good or successful.

6.3 ARGUMENTATION

Here are some obvious points about argumentation that are nonetheless sometimes overlooked.

Typically, an argument for a given claim appeals to further considerations, beyond the claim itself: it is rarely, if ever, the case that asserting a claim is an argument for that claim. In particular, asserting that there are no gods is not an argument for the claim that there are no gods, just as asserting that there are gods is not an argument for the claim that there are gods.

Most people will be inclined to accept that not all claims have *argumentative relevance* to the claim that there are no gods: for example, most people will be inclined to accept that the fact that Chelsea won the 2018 FA Cup is logically, evidentially, and explanatorily irrelevant to the claim that there are no gods. Without any loss of generality, we shall henceforth restrict our attention to claims and beliefs that are logically and/or evidentially and/or explanatorily relevant to the claim or belief that there are no gods.

We said earlier that an atheist is someone who believes, or is committed to, the claim that there are no gods. But no atheist has only the belief that there are no gods; any atheist has many other atheistic beliefs. And, similarly, no theist has only the belief that there is at least one god; every theist has many other theistic beliefs. An argument for atheism or theism that fails to take into account the many other things that atheists and theists believe that are relevant to their atheism or theism may well be seen to be unsuccessful when those further things are taken into account.

It is a commonplace in recent philosophical discussion of belief that we all benefit from and make contributions to *distributed cognitive support*: we all have subject areas where some other people defer to our expertise and we all have subject areas where we defer to the expertise of some others. For all of us, in many subject areas, the justification for much of what we believe is the say-so of those we take to have relevant expertise that we ourselves lack. While this fact is not always properly appreciated, it is a consequence of this distributed cognitive support for our beliefs that our justification for much of what we believe about the merits of arguments about a wide range of subject matters also lies in the say-so of those we take to have relevant expertise. Nobody has the expertise—or the time—to make their own way through all of the sophistical arguments that one could seek out that defend climate change denial, alleged benefits of smoking cigarettes, alleged dangers posed by vaccination against measles, and so forth. Trust in those who we take to be experts to provide us with true beliefs goes hand-in-hand with trust in those we take to be experts to have adequate responses to arguments advanced against the beliefs that we take from those experts. Just as it is proper that assessment of arguments that defend climate change denial, alleged benefits of smoking cigarettes, alleged dangers posed by vaccination against measles, and so forth are handed over to those with expertise in climate science and health science, so, too, assessment of arguments about the existence of gods should be handed over to those with relevant expertise.

Given considerations about distributed cognitive support, it is clear that it is a mistake to think about the virtues of arguments in the context of exchanges between uniformly sampled members of particular populations. People vary enormously in their intelligence, rationality, informedness, interest, sensitivity, and so forth. Doubtless, many people—atheists, agnostics, and theists alike—have ill-informed and/or inconsistent and/or incoherent beliefs about gods. The proper ground of assessment of arguments about the existence of gods adverts to best worldviews and best big pictures across the range of debate. What we really want to know, given arguments for and against the existence of gods, is whether those arguments ought to motivate reconsideration on the part of those who hold best worldviews and best big pictures that incorporate the claims that the arguments target.

If we take the preceding considerations seriously, we arrive at something like the following directives for assessing arguments about the existence of gods. First, we should elaborate best atheistic, agnostic and theistic big pictures, with the same level of care, to the same level of detail. Second, we should check to see whether the arguments that we are assessing show that some of these best big pictures, or their constituent worldviews, suffer from 'internal' deficiencies: inconsistency, incoherence, and the like. Third, for those best big pictures that survive 'internal' scrutiny, we should check to see whether the arguments that we are assessing establish that, in the light of all of the relevant data, some of the remaining best big pictures are more theoretically virtuous than the rest.

If we are making an argument for the 'internal' deficiencies of a competing best big picture, then—as we noted in §5.10.2—we need to make sure that the inconsistency or incoherence that we identify involves claims all of which do belong to best big pictures of the kind that we are attacking, and we need to make sure that those claims really are inconsistent or incoherent.

And, if we are making an argument for the superior theoretical virtue of one kind of best consistent big picture over another, then we need to make sure that we have considered all of the relevant data, that we have not gerrymandered our data, that we have considered all of the relevant theoretical virtues, and that we have properly and fairly assessed the theoretical virtues of the competing best consistent big pictures.

6.4 THEORETICAL VIRTUE

As just noted, the assessment of arguments for the superior theoretical virtue of one kind of best consistent big picture over another requires consideration of all relevant theoretical virtues. But what are relevant theoretical virtues in the assessment of best consistent atheistic, agnostic and theistic big pictures?

While this is a controversial philosophical question, I think that the answer is straightforward: when we assess the comparative theoretical virtues of best consistent big pictures, we are interested in the trade-offs that they make between minimisation of theoretical commitments and maximisation of explanatory breadth and depth.

Theoretical commitments come in various different kinds: ontological, ideological, and nomological. Ontological commitments are commitments to *entities*: minimisation of ontological commitment is minimisation of the numbers and kinds of entities to which big pictures are committed. Ideological commitments are commitments to *ideas*: minimisation of ideological commitment is minimisation of the numbers and kinds of primitive ideas that are used in the framing of big pictures. Nomological commitments are commitments to *principles*: minimisation of nomological commitment is minimisation of the numbers, kinds and complexity of fundamental principles used in the framing of big pictures. Overall, minimisation of theoretical commitments of big pictures is minimisation of numbers and kinds of entities to which big pictures are committed and minimisation of numbers and kinds of primitive ideas and numbers, kinds and complexity of fundamental principles used in the framing of big pictures.

Explanatory breadth and depth also has a number of different dimensions: how much data is left totally unexplained; how much data is poorly explained; how much data is well-explained; how much data is completely explained; and so on. Overall, maximisation of explanatory breadth and depth of big pictures is a matter of explaining as much as possible, as well as possible.

Trade-offs between minimisation of theoretical commitment and maximisation of explanatory breadth and depth can be effected in various ways. At one extreme, if you embrace ontological, ideological, and nomological *nihilism*—so that you are committed to no entities, ideas or principles—then, while your theory scores as well as possible on the count of minimisation of theoretical commitment, it also has no explanatory breadth or depth, and so scores as badly as possible on the count of maximisation of explanatory breadth and depth. At the other extreme, if you embrace an explanatory *particularism* that, in every case, postulates new entities, ideas and principles that yield complete explanations of data, then, while your theory will score as well as possible on the count of maximisation of explanatory breadth and depth, it will score as badly as possible on the count of minimisation of theoretical commitments. While there is no algorithm that tells us when we have achieved the best possible trade-off between minimisation of theoretical commitment and maximisation of explanatory breadth and depth, it is clear that, if there is a best possible trade-off, it will lie somewhere between the extremes of nihilism and particularism.

Given that assessing trade-offs between minimisation of theoretical commitment and maximisation of explanatory breadth and depth can be so fraught, you might be sceptical whether we can ever apply this method. Fortunately, there are some clear cases. Suppose for example, that, when we compare two theories T1 and T2, we find that T2 is committed to everything to which T1 is committed, and more besides, but that there is no data that T2 explains better than T1. In that case, we can clearly conclude that T1 is theoretically more virtuous than T2: there are entities and/or ideas and/or principles to which T2 is committed but to which T1 is committed, and yet commitment to those entities and/or ideas and/or principles does nothing to improve the explanations that are offered by T2. In these circumstances, there is simply no reason to accept those additional entities and/or ideas and/or principles: we should all prefer T1 to T2.

6.5 *ATHEISM IS THE DEFAULT POSITION*

Some atheists claim that there is an initial *presumption* in favour of atheism: before we turn to consider data, we should suppose that there are no gods. Some atheists claim that there is a *burden of proof* that falls on theists: unless theists can point to sufficient reasons—compelling evidence, cogent arguments—that support the claim that there are gods, theists have no entitlement to that belief; but atheists are under no corresponding obligation to point to sufficient reasons—evidence, arguments—that support the claim that there are no gods. Sometimes, it is said that what is true for the idea that there are gods is true for existence claims in general: there is an initial presumption against all existence claims—i.e. claims of the form *there are Fs*—and a burden of proof that falls upon those who wish to defend existence claims.

All of these claims are mistaken. In §6.4 we noted that, when we assess the comparative theoretical virtues of best consistent big pictures, we are interested in the trade-offs that they make between minimisation of theoretical commitments and maximisation of explanatory breadth and depth. While this claim means that we *are* interested in the minimisation of theoretical commitments—and, in particular, that we are interested in minimising the number of claims of the form *there are Fs* that we accept—we are also interested in maximisation of explanatory breadth and depth. Moreover, what we really want to do is to make the best trade-off between minimisation of theoretical commitments and maximisation of explanatory breadth and depth. There is nothing in this methodological framework that says, of particular claims of the form *there are Fs*, that, prior to consideration of the total relevant data, we should expect that they do—or that they do not—belong to the very best consistent big pictures. There is no initial presumption against existence claims; we can be sure, in advance of consideration of data, that the very best consistent big pictures will include lots of existence claims. Moreover, there is no burden of proof that falls asymmetrically upon those who accept certain existence claims: rather, no matter which consistent big picture we favour, we are all subject to the obligation to make the best trade-off between minimisation of theoretical commitments and max-imisation of explanatory breadth and depth.

6.6 *THEISM IS MEANINGLESS*

Ayer (1936: 158) claims that the sentence *there are gods* has 'no lit-eral significance'. According to Ayer's verificationist theory of meaning, there are only two kinds of literally significant sentences: those that express 'analytic truths'—truths of logic, truths of mathematics, truths so solely in virtue of the meanings of words— and those for which there are actual or possible observations that are relevant to the determination of their truth or falsity. Applying his theory, Ayer claims, first, that *there are gods* is not true in virtue of meaning, and, second, that there are no actual or possible observations that are relevant to the truth or falsity of *there are gods*.

Few dispute the claim that *there are gods* is not true in virtue of meaning; however, many deny that there are no actual or possible observations that are relevant to the truth or falsity of *there are gods*. Some theists claim to have made observations that directly support theism; indeed, some claim to have perceived gods. Many people, theists and atheists alike, claim to have described possible courses of experience that would directly support theism. Of course, some atheists deny that there are any such possible courses of experience. But an argument that contains the premise that there are no possible courses of experience that are relevant to the truth or falsity of *there are gods* cannot show that there is an 'internal' problem with those theistic world-views that accept that there are possible observations that would directly support theism and/or that there are actual observations that directly support theism.

Ayer's claim that there are only two kinds of literally significant sentences has very few supporters among contemporary philoso-phers. While it would take us too far afield to explore this matter, it is worth noting that Ayer's objection to theism simply lapses if his verificationist theory of meaning is rejected. Moreover, it is also worth noting that, by Ayer's own lights, if the claim that there are gods is meaningless, then so, too, is the claim that there are no gods. So, if we follow Ayer's own view of things, his argument cannot offer support for atheism.

Perhaps it is worth noting that we might not follow Ayer on this last point; we might suppose, instead, that, if it is true that the sentence there are gods has no literal significance, then it follows that the claim that there are no gods is true. If we take this view, then Ayer's assumptions do, indeed, entail that there are no gods. But, unless best theistic big pictures include both the claim that Ayer's verificationist theory of meaning is correct and the claim that there are no possible courses of experience that are relevant to the truth or falsity of *there are gods*, this entailment yields no reason at all to suppose that there is a serious 'internal' challenge to best theistic big pictures.

6.7 BEST THEISTIC WORLDVIEWS ARE LOGICALLY INCONSISTENT

Some suppose that every best theistic worldview is logically inconsistent: every best theistic worldview contains a set of claims that are jointly logically inconsistent.

Here is an example of the style of argumentation that might be employed by someone who holds this view. Consider the claim that God is omnipotent. Ask yourself: Can God make a stone so heavy that God cannot lift it? Clearly, it is a truth of logic that either God can make a stone so heavy that God cannot lift it or else God cannot make a stone so heavy that God cannot lift it. Equally clearly, it is a truth of logic that an omnipotent being can do anything at all. If God cannot make a stone so heavy that God cannot lift it, then there is something that God cannot do, and so God is not omnipotent. And if God can make a stone so heavy that God cannot lift it, then there is something that God cannot do—namely, lift the stone in question—and so God is not omnipotent. No matter what, then, God is not omnipotent: as a matter of logic, it cannot be that God is omnipotent. So, any best theistic worldview that contains the claim that God is omnipotent is logically inconsistent.

The particular argument that I have just given can be contested on at least two grounds. *First*, it seems wrong to say that it is a truth of logic that an omnipotent being can do anything at all. Most—but not quite all—theists have supposed that not even God can do what it is logically impossible for anything to do. But it is logically impossible for there to be a stone so heavy that an omnipotent being cannot lift it. So the fact that God cannot make a stone so heavy that God cannot lift it poses no threat to the claim that God is omnipotent. And, *second*, it is not clear that it is right to say that, if God can make a stone so heavy that God cannot lift it, then there is something that God cannot do. Perhaps, while God is omnipotent, God could do things that would cause God to cease to be omnipotent; perhaps one of those things would be to make a stone that is so heavy that God cannot lift it. But, even if so, unless God actually makes such a stone, there is no reason to say that God is not omnipotent.

Even if this particular argument were successful, it would only show that all best theistic worldviews are logically inconsistent if all best theistic worldviews contain the claim that God is omnipotent. But it is far from obvious that all best theistic worldviews do contain the claim that God is omnipotent. Certainly, best polytheistic worldviews do not contain the claim that God is omnipotent. Moreover, there are many contemporary monotheists who deny that God is omnipotent; see, for example, Nagasawa (2017). If there are best theistic worldviews that do not include the claim that God is omnipotent, then, of course, there is no prospect that the above argument shows that best theistic worldviews are logically inconsistent.

It is obvious that it is possible to develop logically consistent theistic worldviews. Given that logical inconsistency is such a serious deficit, it is more or less certain that best theistic worldviews are not logically inconsistent. Of course, this leaves it open whether some currently widely accepted theistic worldviews are logically inconsistent. However, even if there are widely accepted theistic worldviews that are logically inconsistent, pointing this out is a very minor win for atheists; as the example provided by Nagasawa (2017) suggests, it is overwhelmingly likely that any logical inconsistency in theistic worldviews can be overcome with relatively minor tinkering.

6.8 BEST THEISTIC BIG PICTURES ARE LOGICALLY INCONSISTENT

Some suppose that every best theistic big picture is logically inconsistent; every best theistic big picture contains a set of claims that are jointly logically inconsistent.

Here is an example of the style of argumentation that might be employed by someone who holds this view. Consider the following set of claims:

1   God exists.
2   God is omnipotent.
3   God is perfectly good.
4   There are no limits to what an omnipotent being can do.
5   A good being eliminates evil as far as it can.
6   Evil exists.

It is clear that this set of claims is jointly logically inconsistent. Given that there are no limits to what an omnipotent being can do, and given that a good being eliminates evil as far as it can, a perfectly good omnipotent being eliminates evil entirely. Hence, if there is an omnipotent perfectly good God, there is no evil. But there is an omnipotent perfectly good God. So there is no evil. But there is evil. So there is evil and there is no evil. Contradiction!

Whether this argument poses a threat to best theistic big pictures depends upon whether best theistic big pictures include *all* of 1–6. Perhaps unsurprisingly, it is doubtful whether there have ever been theists who accept all of 1–6. Certainly, among contemporary theists who accept both that there is a perfectly good omnipotent being and that there is evil, there is little enthusiasm for either the claim that there are no limits to what an omnipotent being can do or for the claim that a good being eliminates evil as far as it can. Many contemporary theists suppose (a) that a good being strives both to promote good and to eliminate evil; (b) that there are at least logical limits on what an omnipotent being can do; and (c) that it is a logical requirement on the existence of certain kinds of important goods that there are evils: for example, there cannot be overcoming of adversity if there is no adversity to overcome. But no theist who accepts (a)–(c) also accepts 4 and 5; and no theists who accept (a)–(c) and who do not accept 4 and 5 is in any way threatened by the observation that 1–6 are jointly logically inconsistent.

The lesson here is much like the lesson in §6.7: it is obvious that it is possible to develop logically consistent theistic big pictures. Because logical inconsistency is such a serious deficit, it is more or less certain that best theistic big pictures are not logically inconsistent. Of course, it may be that there are widely accepted inconsistent theistic big pictures. But, even if that is so, it is not hugely significant: relatively minor tinkering will remove logical inconsistency from inconsistent theistic big pictures.

6.9 BEST THEISTIC BIG PICTURES ARE INFERIOR TO BEST ATHEISTIC BIG PICTURES

All minimally rational atheists suppose that best theistic big pictures are inferior to best atheistic big pictures. However, only some atheists suppose that there are arguments that ought to persuade everyone to adopt an atheistic big picture. As we noted in §2.4, some atheists suppose that there can be reasonable disagreement, between thoughtful, reflective, sufficiently intelligent, sufficiently well-informed people, about the existence of gods. Those atheists suppose that there are no arguments that ought to persuade everyone to adopt an atheistic big picture; those atheists suppose that it is simply a matter for judgment whether one favours a theistic big picture, or one favours an atheistic big picture, or one favours neither theistic big pictures nor atheistic big pictures.

How might one try to argue that best theistic big pictures are inferior to best atheistic big pictures, given that one does not adopt any of the strategies discussed in §§6.5–6.8? In my view, the most plausible way to proceed is to argue for the following two claims: (a) best atheistic big pictures have fewer theoretical commitments than best theistic big pictures; and (b) there is no data that theistic big pictures explain better than atheistic big pictures. From these two claims, given the account of theoretical virtue in §6.4, it follows that best atheistic big pictures are superior to best theistic big pictures.

6.9.1 FEWER THEORETICAL COMMITMENTS

In order to argue that best atheistic big pictures have fewer theoretical commitments than best theistic big pictures, we need to argue (i) that best atheistic big pictures are less ontologically committing than best theistic big pictures; (ii) that best atheistic big pictures are less ideologically committing than best theistic big pictures; and (iii) that best atheistic big pictures are less nomologically committing than best theistic big pictures.

The basic argument in each case is very straightforward. Setting gods aside, best atheistic big pictures and best theistic big pictures agree in their ontological, ideological, and nomological commitments. If, for example, natural reality is a distribution of fields over a manifold, then best atheistic big pictures and best theistic big pictures agree in the ontological, ideological and nomological commitments that are required by the claim that natural reality is a distribution of fields over a manifold. More generally, the content of natural scientific knowledge, human scientific knowledge, formal scientific knowledge, applied scientific knowledge, humanistic knowledge, and artistic knowledge is independent of the question of the existence of god. Objects, ideas and principles that are required for the best formulations of the natural sciences, the human sciences, the formal sciences, the applied sciences, the humanities and the arts are common to best atheistic big pictures and best theistic big pictures. But best theistic big pictures—unlike best atheistic big pictures—require more: their commitment to gods, and their allied commitment to ideas and principles that apply only to gods, has no counterpart in best atheistic big pictures.

Of course, on its own, this point about theoretical commitments provides no reason to favour atheism over theism. Theists claim that the additional theoretical commitments that come along with their commitment to gods is justified by the explanatory advantages that accrue when we consider the comparative merits of atheistic and theistic explanations of the relevant data. The key question, still to be addressed, is whether there is data that is better explained in best theistic big pictures than in best atheistic big pictures.

6.9.2 EXPLANATORY PARITY

In order to make a proper assessment of the comparative merits of atheistic and theistic big picture explanations of data, we need to make sure that we consider *all* of the relevant data. If we allow ourselves to cherry pick, we can surely assemble data sets that favour our own preferred view. For example, considered in isolation, the fact that there have been, and are, many thoughtful, reflective, intelligent, well-informed theists provides some support for the claim that best big pictures are best theistic big pictures. But, when we consider a wider range of facts about the full spectrum of human opinion about gods—including the fact that there have been, and are, many thoughtful, reflective, intelligent, well-informed atheists, and the fact that there is endless disagreement among thoughtful, reflective, intelligent, well-informed theists about the number and nature of gods—it becomes clear that the facts about the distribution of opinion do not favour the claim that best big pictures are best theistic big pictures.

In §5.10.3, I argued that the existence of natural reality is not better explained in best theistic big pictures than it is in best atheistic big pictures. Sure, on a narrow view, it looks as though the existence of natural reality has an explanation on best theistic big pictures, and no explanation on best atheistic big pictures, and this looks like an explanatory advantage for best theistic big pictures. But appearances here are deceptive. Best theistic big pictures and best atheistic big pictures give the same account of the existence of causal reality; they merely disagree about additional items that only theists think belong to causal reality. Given that, in best atheistic big pictures, natural reality has the same standing that causal reality has in best theistic big pictures, it is clearly a mistake to suppose that the claim that natural reality is the product of divine creative activity confers some kind of relative explanatory advantage on best theistic big pictures.

In §5.10.3, I gave a partial list of what is alleged to be data that favours best theistic big pictures over best atheistic big pictures: (a) our part of natural reality is fine-tuned for our existence; (b) there are irreducibly complex biological entities; (c) there are reliable reports of divine intervention in human history; (d) we are capable of logical, mathematical and statistical reasoning; (e) we have modal knowledge; (f) we have moral knowledge; (g) we are moved by the dictates of conscience; (h) we are capable of appreciating beauty; (i) we are (sometimes) conscious; (j) there are reliable reports of direct experience of the divine; (k) there are scriptures that record important truths about the divine; (l) we have a capacity for humour; and (m) we have a capacity for love. I can do no more here than make some brief remarks that indicate how atheists might argue that the various pieces of data do not support best theistic big pictures over best atheistic big pictures.

Some, but not all, cosmologists suppose that our universe is *fine-tuned*: had the values of various physical constants been ever-so-slightly different, either our universe would have existed for no more than a few seconds, or else it would always have consisted of nothing but empty space; and, either way, it would not have contained atoms, molecules, proteins, plants, animals, human beings, oceans, planets, stars, galaxies and so on. When we think about possible explanations for the fine-tuning of our part of causal reality, there are two cases to consider. On the one hand, it may be that, at every prior point in causal reality, it is already fixed that—absent subsequent intervention—our universe is fine-tuned. On the other hand, it may be that there is some point in causal reality prior to which is it not fixed that—absent subsequent intervention—our universe is be fine-tuned, but after which it is fixed that—absent subsequent intervention—our universe is fine-tuned. If it is true at every point in causal reality that—absent subsequent intervention—our universe is fine-tuned, then there are four different claims that we might make about the fine-tuning (cf. §5.10.3): ultimately, our universe is fine-tuned because it *must* be; ultimately, our universe is fine-tuned because it *always* has been; ultimately, our universe is fine-tuned because it is *good* that it is; ultimately, our universe is fine-tuned for *no further reason* of any kind. And if it is true that there is a point prior to which our universe is not fine-tuned but after which it is, then, ultimately, our universe is fine-tuned as a matter of *chance*: it underwent a transition from not being fine-tuned to being fine-tuned without there being anything that required this transition to take place. Since *all* of these explanations are available in equal measure to atheists and theists, there is nothing in considerations about fine-tuning that supports best theistic big pictures over best atheistic big pictures.

Some theists have argued, and continue to argue, that the cornerstone of the modern life sciences—biological evolution by way of natural selection—is unable to provide a complete account of the developmental pathway from the simplest organisms that populated the earth billions of years ago to the diverse complex organisms that our planet has housed in the much more recent past. One of the best known arguments of this kind appeals to cases of *irreducible complexity*: cases in which slight modifications in *any* components of complex systems cause catastrophic loss of function. If current organisms contain irreducibly complex systems, then, on this line of thought, those organisms could not have arisen as a result of biological evolution by way of natural selection, because the relevant systems in the hypothesised immediately ancestral organisms would have been non-functional. This line of thought depends upon the mistaken supposition that biological evolution by way of natural selection is always a matter of slight modification at all levels in the organism. However, while it is true that biological evolution by way of natural selection is typically a matter of minor modification at the genetic level—the addition or deletion of a single protein, or the relocation of a single sequence of proteins—it is not true that biological evolution by way of natural selection is always a matter of minor modification at higher levels of the organism. There is almost universal consensus among biological experts that irreducible complexity can arise, and has arisen, in the course of biological evolution by way of natural selection; there is almost universal consensus among biological experts that biological evolution by way of natural selection pro- vides a complete account of the development of life on earth. Given all of this, we should not think that considerations about irreducible complexity give best theistic big pictures an explanatory advantage over best atheistic big pictures; rather, we should sup- pose that best atheistic big pictures and best theistic big pictures both accept that biological evolution by way of natural selection provides a complete account of the development of life on earth.

It is, of course, true that human beings have capacities for humour, love, aesthetic appreciation, moral reasoning, modal rea- soning, statistical reasoning, mathematical reasoning, logical rea- soning, moral knowledge, modal knowledge, statistical knowledge, mathematical knowledge, logical knowledge, and so forth. But it is also true that human capacities for these kinds of things are subject to many kinds of curious limitations. For example, in §4.1, we noted that psychologists take advantage of our propensity to commit the conjunction fallacy in order to probe the stereotypes that we use in making judgments about classes of people. More broadly, recent psychological research has disclosed a wide range of ways in which we are all disposed to quite elementary lapses in our logical reasoning, mathematical reasoning, statistical reasoning, moral reasoning, and the like (see Kahneman 2011). When we consider the full range of relevant data, it is overwhelmingly plausible that those capacities *and their limitations* are fully explained by billions of years of biological evolution and millions of year of cultural development. But, if that's right, then best atheistic big pictures and best theistic big pictures tell exactly the same story about the capacities of human beings, and there is no explanatory advantage that accrues on either side as a result of consideration of this data.

Some theists have argued that considerations about religious experience, scripture and miracles supports best theistic big pictures over best atheistic big pictures. It is important to be clear about what the data is here. We have numerous reports—from all of the religions of the earth—concerning miracles and religious experiences, each of which is alleged to support exactly one of those religions. Moreover, we have scriptures belonging to all of the religions of the earth, each of which is alleged to support exactly one of those religions. Everyone—no matter which big picture they espouse—supposes that almost all of the reports of miracles and religious experiences, and almost all of the scriptures, do not give support to the religions to which they are claimed to give support; everyone *explains away* almost all of the reports of miracles and religious experience, and almost all of the scriptures. But, in that case, atheists are among those uniquely well-placed to give a uniform account of all reports of miracles and religious experiences and all scriptures; atheists explain them all away in exactly the manner that, for example, theists explain away everything except the data they take to support their own theistic religion. Since atheists have a uniform account, and since it must be that there is an enormous amount of special pleading among those who do not have a uniform account, it is reasonable to accept that there is no explanatory advantage that accrues to those theists who advert to considerations about religious experience, scripture and miracles: best atheistic big pictures cannot do worse than best theistic big pictures in managing these considerations.

6.9.3 *SUMMATION AND ASSESSMENT*

The form of the argument for atheism that I have been sketching is clear. Best atheistic big pictures have fewer theoretical commitments than best theistic big pictures, but there is nowhere that best theistic big pictures provide better explanations than best atheistic big pictures. So, best atheistic big pictures are more theoretically virtuous than best theistic big pictures, and so should be preferred to them.

Of course, I have done no more than sketch how such an argument might go; I certainly haven not tried to give an argument of this kind. As it stands, almost everything in the sketch that I have given is contestable. Perhaps it is not true that best atheistic big pictures have fewer theoretical commitments than best theistic big pictures. Perhaps it is not true that there is nowhere that best theistic big pictures provide better explanations than best atheistic big pictures. Perhaps the account of theoretical virtue upon which the sketch relies is mistaken: perhaps there are theoretical virtues other than minimisation of theoretical commitments and maximisation of explanatory breadth and depth.

However, be all that as it may, it seems to me to be clearly right that the kind of argument that I have sketched here is the only kind of argument of which it is plausible to suggest that it might succeed in showing that atheism is preferable to agnosticism and theism. Moreover, it also seems to me that, if there is no successful argument of this kind, then there just are no successful arguments for any of atheism, agnosticism and theism. If there is no lining up of judgments about where explanatory advantage lies, then there just is no prospect of the construction of compelling cases for any of these positions.

Perhaps it might be said that, even if the argument I have sketched is not compelling, the framework within which it has been developed can be put to other uses. For example, even if the case is not compelling, the framework within which it has been developed may serve some purpose in demonstrating to others the kinds of judgments that atheists rely upon as justification for their atheism. Moreover, it might be added, agnostics and theists can use the same framework to demonstrate the kinds of judgments that they rely upon in justifying their positions. If we suppose that there is agreement on the claim that best atheistic big pictures have fewer theoretical commitments than best theistic big pictures, and that there is also agreement on the theoretical virtues invoked in the sketched argument, then it must turn out that agnostics are uncertain about whether best theistic big pictures do have explanatory advantages over best atheistic big pictures in a sufficient range of cases, and that theists suppose that best theistic big pictures have an explanatory advantage over best atheistic big pictures in a sufficient range of cases. If atheists, agnostics and theists agree to disagree about the range of cases, then perhaps we have everything that it is reasonable to hope for in this domain.

6.10 *CONCLUDING REMARKS*

In this chapter, I have considered and rejected most forms of argument for atheism. I do not accept that atheism is the default position. I do not accept that theism is meaningless. I do not accept that best theistic worldviews are logically inconsistent. I do not accept that best theistic big pictures are logically inconsistent. And, while I do think that best atheistic big pictures are more theoretically virtuous than best theistic big pictures, I am sceptical that anyone will ever be able to write down an argument that succeeds in establishing, to the satisfaction of all interested parties, that this is the case.

7

ON THE ROAD AGAIN

In the previous chapters, we have: considered what atheism is; examined the lives of some historically significant atheists; considered what social science tells us about atheism and atheists; examined a range of criticisms of atheism and atheists; and looked at ways that we might argue for atheism and the views of atheists.

In this, the final chapter, we take up the question where atheism now seems to be headed. This question is much disputed. Some think that atheism is currently booming, and that it will continue to grow rapidly into the future. Others think that atheism is now in decline, and that it will wither away in the coming years.

The dispute about where atheism is headed is fought on at least two different fronts. One front is *empirical*, and concerns what the social scientific data that we have are telling us about the likely demographic future of atheism. Another front is *conceptual*: it focusses on what the current state of debate and theorising may tell us about the likely intellectual future of atheism.

We start with consideration of reasons commonly taken to support the claim that atheism is currently booming.

7.1 THE 'NEW' ATHEISM

The first couple of decades of the third millennium has seen a boom in the sales of 'new' atheist books. Consider, for example, Ali (2008), Christina (2016), Dawkins (2006), Dennett (2006), Goldberg (2007), Grayling (2007), Harris (2004), Hecht (2003), Hitchens (2007), Jacoby (2005), Kaminer (2000), Onfray (2007),

Pataki (2007), Stenger (2007), and numerous others. These works are typically atheistic, naturalistic, and anti-religious.

The rise of 'new' atheist literature has coincided with a wave of 'new' atheist activism. There have been films: Dawkins's *The Root of all Evil?*; Bill Maher's *Religulous*; and Theo von Gogh's *Submission*. There have been publicity stunts, such as the Atheist Bus Campaign, launched initially in the UK, but followed with similar ventures in Australia, Brazil, Canada, Finland, Germany, Ireland, Italy, Netherlands, New Zealand, Russia, Spain, Sweden, Switzerland, and the United States. There have been Global Atheist Conventions in Melbourne on 12–14 March 2010 and 13–15 April 2012; interestingly, a follow-up convention scheduled for February 2018, headlined by Salman Rushdie, was cancelled because of 'lack of interest'. And there has been an enormous amount of heated debate and discussion, both online and in more traditional public fora.

Some suppose that the rise of 'new' atheists shows that atheism is ascendant. However, it is not clear that 'new' atheism really has *arisen* in a way that would vindicate this supposition. Since the early 1790s, when Chaumette declared that Christians are enemies of reason and that their ideas are ridiculous, there has been a steady stream of irreligionists whose works and activities have irritated religious believers. In *The Age of Reason*—published in three volumes in 1794, 1795, and 1807—Thomas Paine's repackaging of existing deistic critiques of religion had very broad public appeal: it sold by the bucket load, and provoked numerous intemperate responses. Consider, for example, Watson (1796: 2):

> I hope that there is no want of charity in saying that it would have been fortunate for the Christian world had [Paine's] life been terminated before [he] had fulfilled [his] intention.

The very long list of similar subsequent irritants includes, for example, Ingersoll (1872), Foote (1886), Gage (1893), Stanton (1895), McCabe (1917), Cohen (1921), Haldeman-Julius (1926), Lewis (1954), Russell (1957), and Kurtz (1987). Here is a small sample from Ingersoll which shows just how little rhetorical difference there is between our 'new' atheists and freethinkers from the middle of the nineteenth century:

The trouble is, these pious people shut up their reason and open their Bible.

(Ingersoll 1872: 33)

We have listened to all the drowsy, idealess, vapid sermons that we wish to hear. ... All these amount to less than nothing. ... It is worse than useless to show us fishes with money in their mouths, and call our attention to vast multitudes stuffing themselves with five crackers and two sardines.

(Ingersoll 1872: 52)

To prevent famine, one plan is worth a million sermons, and even patent medicines will cure more diseases than all the prayers uttered since the beginning of the world.

(Ingersoll 1872: 61)

The originality of repetition, and the mental vigour of acquiescence, are all that we have any right to expect from the Christian world.

(Ingersoll 1872: 63)

Basking in the sunshine of a delusion ... the world was filled with ignorance, superstition and misery.

(Ingersoll 1872: 65)

The civilisation of man has increased to just the same extent that religious power has decreased.

(Ingersoll 1872: 78)

Of course, then—as now—not all atheists embraced the confrontational approach taken by Paine, Ingersoll, and others. As we noted in §3.7 and §3.9—in our discussions of Mary Ann Evans and Eric Blair—there have been atheists who are sympathetic to religion and, at least in the West, to Christianity. Whether the proportion of contemporary atheists who are sympathetic to the 'new' atheists is greater than the proportion of atheists in previous generations who resonated with their corresponding public confrontationists is not at all clear. It is worth bearing in mind that, in 1800, the population of the world was no more than 900 million, of whom 5 million lived in the United States; in 2017, the population of the world is 7.5 billion, of whom 325 million live in the United States. Even if the relative number of atheists has not increased, there are orders of magnitude more atheists in the United States in 2017 than there were in 1800. Moreover, with the rise of the Internet and social media, a much greater percentage of people have access to means of publicly airing their views. So there is clearly room for wondering whether the proportion of contemporary atheists who are sympathetic to the 'new' atheists is greater than the proportion of atheists in previous generations who resonated with their corresponding public confrontationists; and there is also room for wondering whether the coming to prominence of the 'new' atheists really does coincide with a genuine rise in the fortunes of atheism.

Flynn (2012) says:

> There's nothing new about the New Atheism. ... Readers familiar with nineteenth and twentieth century freethought literature ... know that everything the [New Atheists] are being praised and condemned for have been done before. Well. Many times. Throughout the nineteenth and twentieth centuries, articulate writers have declared religion untrue, faith a social evil, and the archetypal stories told by the world's great creeds nothing but clumsy legends. ... The triumph of [the New Atheists] is to take arguments against religion that have long been familiar to insiders, brilliantly repackage them, and expose them to millions who would never otherwise pick up an atheist book. That's no small achievement.

This doesn't seem quite right. As I have already noted, from the time of Thomas Paine there have been writers who have taken up arguments against religion familiar to insiders and repackaged them for a wider public. But the arguments that are in circulation among insiders do change over time. Later generations have more relevant scientific knowledge than earlier generations, including knowledge spawned by fields that have only recently come into existence: for example, much recent atheistic and naturalistic theorising about religion is based on what Atran (2002: vii) calls 'the convergence of evolutionary biology and cognitive psychology'. Moreover, the targets for atheistic and naturalistic critique of religion are not stationary: different generations of religious apologists appeal to different kinds of considerations. It is, I think, more accurate to say that the 'new' atheism of each succeeding generation reworks the atheism of preceding generations in the light of changing circumstances: the basic frameworks remain the same, but there is lots of change in detail.

It is not just that Flynn exaggerates when he claims that there is nothing new about the 'new' atheism; it is also questionable whether what he takes to be the 'triumph' of the 'new' atheists is really very different from the 'triumphs' of atheists in earlier ages. As far as we know, the first publicly circulated atheistic pamphlet in the UK that had its author's name attached to it appeared during the 1770s. Not much more than a century before that, the 1661 UK Act against the Crime of Blasphemy had made it a capital offence to 'obstinately persist' in denial of the existence of God. Under this Act, atheists were to be put to death merely for continuing to express their sincerely held beliefs. From the 1770s, in the UK, courageous publishers and authors succeeded in 'exposing and repackaging' arguments against religion—drawn from Cherbury, Meslier and Hume—to wide audiences who would otherwise not have had access to atheist publications. Set against this background, it is not obvious that there is anything particularly distinctive about the 'triumph' of our 'new' atheists.

There are also questions to be faced about whether our 'new' atheists suffer from shortcomings that did not afflict atheist controversialists in earlier times. Some opponents of our 'new' atheists allege that they are distinctively intolerant and aggressive. In particular, some opponents of our 'new' atheists allege that they have a distinctively negative view of religion founded in crudely 'scientistic' and 'reductionist' views of religion. One theme in much—though by no means all—of the 'new' atheism is that religion is an enemy of both philosophy and reason, a relic of our shameful past that ought to be put down with extreme rancour. Consider:

> The idea ... that religious faith is somehow a sacred human convention—distinguished, as it is, both by the extravagance of its claims and by the paucity of its evidence—is really too great a monstrosity to be appreciated in all its glory. Religious faith represents so

uncompromising a misuse of the power of our minds that it forms a kind of perverse cultural singularity—a vanishing point beyond which rational discourse proves impossible. When foisted upon each generation anew, it renders us incapable of realising just how much of our world has been unnecessarily ceded to a dark and barbarous past.

(Harris 2004: 25)

What is really pernicious is the practice of teaching children that faith itself is a virtue. Faith is an evil precisely because it requires no justification and brooks no argument. Teaching children that unquestioned faith is a virtue primes them—given other ingredients that are not hard to come by—to grow up into potentially lethal weapons for future jihads or crusades. ... Faith can be very, very dangerous, and deliberately to implant it into the vulnerable mind of an innocent child is a grievous wrong.

(Dawkins 2006: 307–309)

While the rise—and excesses—of militant Islam and evangelical Christianity loom large in the imagination of many 'new' atheists, their criticism extends to all manifestations of religious belief:

The greatest problem confronting civilisation is not merely religious extremism: rather, it is the larger set of cultural and intellectual accommodations we have made to faith itself. Religious moderates are, in large part, responsible for the religious conflict in our world, because their beliefs provide the context in which scriptural literalism and religious violence can never be adequately opposed.

(Harris 2004: 45)

As long as we accept the principle that religious faith must be respected simply because it is religious faith, it is hard to withhold respect from the faith of Osama bin Laden and the suicide bombers. The alternative, one so transparent that it should need no urging, is to abandon the principle of automatic respect for religious faith. This is one reason why I do everything in my power to warn people against faith itself, not just against so-called 'extremist' faith. The teachings of 'moderate' religion, though not extremist in themselves, are an open invitation to extremism.

(Dawkins 2006: 306)

In my estimation, the treatment of 'religious moderates' is a—not necessarily unprecedented—blackspot in the works of many 'new' atheists, including Dawkins and Harris. Given the broadly liberal, pluralistic framing of their political views, it is to be expected that the 'new' atheists endorse perfect separation of church and state and keenly support rights to freedom of speech, freedom of assembly, freedom of conscience, and the like. But there are many 'religious moderates' who no less strongly endorse perfect separation of church and state and no less keenly support rights to freedom of speech, freedom of assembly, freedom of conscience, and the like. Any plausible formulation of pluralistic liberalism builds in protection against all kinds of 'extremist' actions: the same basket of rights is available in equal measure to all, and any action—individual or collective—that threatens to deprive some of some measure of some of their rights is properly subject to sanction. The faith of 'religious moderates' who endorse pluralistic liberalism is no invitation to extremism and bears no responsibility for religious conflict; indeed, pluralistic liberalism has its origins in the designs of 'religious moderates' to bring an end to the ruinous religious conflicts that wracked Europe during the sixteenth century. Of course, it is to be expected that pluralistic liberal atheists will protest vociferously if there is less than perfect separation of church and state; and the historical record is replete with examples of atheists making loud protests of this kind. Moreover, it is to be expected that some pluralistic liberal atheists will use their freedom of expression to vigorously criticise what they take to be the religious beliefs of religious moderates; such vigorous criticism is par for the course under pluralistic liberalism. But it seems to me to be serious confusion for pluralistic liberal atheists to suppose that it is impossible for 'religious moderates' to be citizens of a pluralistic liberal state.

While, as the preceding paragraph shows, I think that there are serious criticisms of some of the views of some of the 'new' atheists, I doubt that the 'new' atheists suffer from shortcomings that did not afflict atheist controversialists in earlier times. To the extent that it is true that the 'new' atheists expose and repackage arguments that have long been familiar to insiders, it is equally true that all participants in public debates expose and repackage arguments that have long been familiar to insiders. Moreover, ever since there has been public dispute between theists and atheists, there have been theists who have accused atheists of 'scientism', and 'reductionism', and intolerance, and rudeness, and the like. If we are interested in determining whether atheism is flourishing, it is not clear that we will learn much simply from consideration of the words and deeds of current atheist controversialists.

7.2 INSIDE THE ACADEMY

There are some academics from a range of disciplines who claim that theism is on the rise—and, hence, that atheism is in decline—within the academy. In particular, we can find philosophers, theologians, and sociologists who claim that the atheistic sun is vanishing beneath the horizon. I shall consider one example from each of these disciplines in turn.

7.2.1 PHILOSOPHY

According to the introduction to Craig and Moreland (2009: ix):

> The face of Anglo-American philosophy has been transformed. ... Theism is on the rise; atheism is on the decline. Atheism, although perhaps still the dominant viewpoint at the American university, is a philosophy in retreat.

Craig (undated) adds details to what has become, in some philosophical circles, an oft-told triumphalist narrative:

> In recent times, the battlelines have dramatically shifted. ... Undoubtedly the most important philosophical event of the twentieth century was the collapse of the verificationism that lay at the heart of scientific naturalism. ... The collapse of verificationism brought with it a ... disillusionment with the whole Enlightenment project of scientific naturalism. ... In philosophy the demise of verificationism has been accompanied by a resurgence of metaphysics, ... the birth of a new

discipline, philosophy of religion, and a renaissance in Christian philosophy. ... Since the late 1960s, Christian philosophers have been out of the closet and defending the truth of the Christian worldview with philosophically sophisticated arguments in the finest scholarly journals and professional societies. ... Today, philosophy of religion flourishes in young journals ... not to mention the standard non-specialist journals. ... Philosophy departments are a beachhead from which operations can be launched to impact other disciplines at the university for Christ.

This triumphalist narrative is massively implausible. The percentage of the US population that is Christian has declined significantly since the 1960s even though the population has doubled. Moreover, there have been huge increases in undergraduate and postgraduate participation in US universities; as a result, access to higher education, employment opportunities in universities, and so forth, have grown at a much faster rate than the decline in participation in the Christian religion. Atheism is much more prevalent in philosophy than in just about all other academic disciplines. Nonetheless, for a whole host of reasons—absolute increase in number of Christians in philosophy, vast array of new philosophy journals, dramatic improvements in air travel and communication, etc.—it would be astonishing if, since the 1960s, Christian philosophers in the US had not managed to establish some new societies, found some new journals, run some new conferences and workshops, and so forth. Moreover, there is less philosophy of religion being published in flagship philosophy journals (e.g. *Mind*) than there was in the 1960s, and there is less philosophy of religion at major US universities (e.g. Princeton, Yale, Harvard) than there was in the 1960s (for the relevant details, see Oppy forthcoming). The unsurprising upshot is that there is simply no evidence that supports the wishful thinking that is displayed in the triumphalist narrative. Moreover, there is evidence that appears to count against the triumphalist narrative. For example, according to the *PhilPapers* 2009 survey (https://philpapers.org/surveys/results.pl) just 14.6 per cent of US professional philosophers accept or lean towards theism; it strains credulity to suppose that a smaller percentage of US professional philosophers accepted or leant towards theism in the 1960s.

7.2.2 *THEOLOGY*

McGrath (2004: 279) claims that atheism is in a 'twilight zone'. In his view:

> The simple fact is that interest in religion has grown globally since the high-water mark of secularism in the 1970s, even in the heartlands of the West. ... This new interest in things spiritual has swept through Western culture in the last decade. ... In what follows, we shall explore ... the observed waning appeal of atheism.
>
> (McGrath 2004: 190–192)

It is an interesting question what observations McGrath made in the years prior to the writing of this book. Clearly, he did not look at the demographic data. In all countries with relatively high gross domestic product per capita, there have been declines in religious affiliation and religiosity over a period of many decades. Moreover, those trends have accelerated in the decade and a half since McGrath's book appeared. McGrath's offhand remarks about 'the change in direction of the long-running television series Star Trek' (McGrath 2004: 190) after Gene Roddenberry's death in 1991 and 'the burgeoning bookstore sections dealing with "Body, Mind and Spirit"' (McGrath 2004: 191) hardly constitute a serious counterweight. At the very least, in order to take these remarks with any degree of seriousness, we need to be told about trends in *other* bookstore sections and television series; there has, after all, been an interesting line in 'new' atheist texts and films that was burgeoning at the time that McGrath's book went to press.

While McGrath claims to have empirical data on his side, it is possible that he takes the main part of his case to rest in theoretical considerations. McGrath offers a three-pronged argument for the conclusion that the intellectual foundations for atheism have collapsed. First, the intellectual case against God is weak: the arguments of Feuerbach, Marx and Freud are all *post hoc* rationalisations that presuppose the atheism that they set out to vindicate (McGrath 2004: 179–182); and, in any case, postmodernism subjects atheism to devastating deconstructive critique (McGrath 2004: 227–237). Second, the course of history in the twentieth century overthrows any claims that atheism might have to being an agent of political and intellectual liberation (McGrath 2004: 258–264). And, third, atheism is wishy-washy and unexciting: dull, dated, and grey (McGrath 2004: 269–273). All of these considerations are extraordinarily weak.

Although McGrath correctly claims that theories developed by Feuerbach, Marx and Freud assume atheism, and hence cannot be used as *direct* arguments for atheism, it is (a) a mistake to suppose that empirical support for those theories could not yield indirect arguments for atheism; and (b) a much more serious error to suppose that the best available arguments for atheism rely heavily upon those theories for either direct or indirect support. While it is doubtful that there is independent support for the theories of Feuerbach, Marx, and Freud, it is clear that, if there were independent support for those theories, then that would also be support for atheism. But, in any case, examination of the best recent arguments for atheism—in, for example, Mackie (1982) and Sobel (2004)—immediately discloses that it is not at all plausible to dismiss those best arguments for atheism as *post hoc* rationalisations. Look back at the argument that was set out in §6.9: that argument does not presuppose the atheism that it sets out to vindicate, and nor does it have any truck with the theories developed by Feuerbach, Marx and Freud. In short: McGrath's first set of considerations provides no reason at all to suppose that intellectual foundations for atheism have collapsed.

The claim that postmodernism subjects atheism to devastating deconstructive critique is, at best, highly controversial. Very roughly, *postmodernism* is an intellectual movement that yields a negative—sceptical, ironic—assessment of 'grand narratives' and 'universalist ideologies' and promotes a tendency towards relativist and pluralist construals of truth and knowledge. Equally roughly, *deconstruction* is a method of textual analysis that focuses on ways in which 'grand narratives' and 'universalist ideologies' are undone by their own presuppositions and frames of reference. Given that best theistic big pictures are no less candidates to be 'grand narratives' and 'universalist ideologies' than best atheistic big pictures, it is not in the least bit plausible that only best theistic big pictures survive deconstructive critique. It seems true that current 'post-theological' thinkers (e.g. Alan Badiou, Jean-Luc Nancy, and Quentin Meillassoux) debate the possibility of arriving at a consistent formulation of what they consider to be atheism (see Watkin 2011); but it is simply not on the cards that the upshot of that debate is a vindication of familiar forms of theism.

McGrath's objection to atheism on the ground of the course of history in the twentieth century should be considered alongside the objection to theism on the ground of the course of history in the past forty centuries. Should we suppose that the course of history in the past forty centuries supports the claim that theism is a greater agent of intellectual and political liberation than atheism? If the horrors perpetrated by communist regimes in the twentieth century are to be laid at the feet of atheism, then the horrors perpetrated by other regimes in the past forty centuries are, with equal justice, to be laid at the feet of theism. There is nothing more in the claim that there are no gods than there is in the claim that there are gods that lends support to slaughter and carnage. It would be a brave soul who bet that, over the course of history, it is only a minority who have engaged in slaughter and carnage while believing that the gods are on their side.

The claim that atheism is wishy-washy, unexciting, dull, dated and grey is odd. When we compare the claim that there are gods with the claim that there are no gods, it is very hard to discern any reason for thinking that one of these claims is less wishy-washy, unexciting, dull, dated and grey than the other. Since there is nothing more to being an atheist than believing that there are no gods, and nothing more to being a theist than believing that there is at least one god, it is hard to see any reason to accept that theists are less wishy-washy, unexciting, dull, dated and grey than atheists. Of course, it might be that—in particular places, at particular times—there is an accidental connection between, say, theism, and wishy-washiness, lack of excitement, dullness, datedness, and greyness. For example, in the US, right now, there is a demographic divide: atheism is far more prevalent among the young than among the old. At the very least, we seem on fairly safe grounds if we suggest that, on average, theists are *greyer* in the US right now!

In short: McGrath (2004) offers no serious support for the claim that atheism is in decline in the West. On the one hand, there is no serious demographic study that has been conducted in the past thirty years that supports this contention; and there are many serious demographic studies in that time that are alleged to support the claim that atheism is on the rise. On the other hand, if there are serious intellectual arguments against atheism, McGrath has certainly failed to find them.

7.2.3 SOCIOLOGY

Bouma (2006: 86, 129, 206) writes:

> An examination of both the qualitative and quantitative aspects of Australia's religious and spiritual life shows that they have a healthy future. ... The emerging picture of Australia's religious and spiritual life shows continued vitality. ... Religion and spirituality never engaged everyone's attention or commitment. I expect, however, that more will in the near future than did in the near past.

Bouma's book relies heavily on a comparison of the 1996 and 2001 Australian census data. Some of the data are summarised in (Table 7.1).

If we sum the two columns, we have 25.58 per cent for the 1996 Census and 27.80 per cent for the 2001 Census who did *not* tick boxes that indicates a clear religious identification: Christian (Anglican, Baptist, Catholic, Lutheran, Uniting, Orthodox, Pentecostal, Other), Buddhist, Hindu, Jew, Muslim, Other. We might

Table 7.1 Lack of religious identification, Australia, 1996 and 2001

	1996 census	*2001 census*
No religion	16.48	15.48
Atheist	0.04	0.13
Agnostic	0.05	0.09
Humanist	0.02	0.03
Rationalist	0.01	0.01
Jedi	—	0.40
Not stated	8.67	9.78
Inadequate description	0.31	1.88

suppose that this is evidence of a decline in religiosity between the two censuses. However, Bouma (2006: 55) says:

> The category 'not stated' poses an insurmountable problem of interpretation. Some commentators lump these respondents with those who declare they have 'no religion'; however, that practice is not justifiable. ... Interpreting a non-response poses a serious problem and should be avoided.

Before we jump to the conclusion that Bouma was right to worry about those who fall in the 'not stated' group, it is worth looking at a wider data set. Let's start with the prior censuses conducted by the Australian government (Table 7.2). What is interesting here is the change between 1966 and 1971. It seems to me to be very plausible to interpret this change as a redistribution from 'not stated' to 'no religion'. It's not that the number of those with no religion suddenly had an uncharacteristically large spurt; rather, it's that a whole lot of people who had previously withheld information about their status were now prepared to tick the 'no religion' box. This is at least some indication that a very significant

Table 7.2 Lack of religious identification, Australia, 1911–1991

Year	No religion	Not stated	Inadequate description	Total
1911	0.4	2.7	0.2	3.3
1922	0.5	1.7	0.2	2.4
1933	0.2	12.8	0.1	13.1
1947	0.3	10.9	0.2	11.4
1954	0.3	9.5	0.2	10.0
1961	0.4	10.5	0.2	11.1
1966	0.8	10.0	0.3	11.1
1971	6.7	6.1	0.2	13.0
1976	8.3	11.8	0.4	20.5
1981	10.8	10.9	0.5	22.2
1986	12.7	11.9	0.5	24.9
1991	12.9	10.5	0.3	23.7

proportion of those who withheld information in the 1966 census actually had no religion.

We can also look at the subsequent censuses conducted by the Australian government (Table 7.3). Since the 1966 census there has been a clear upward trend in those ticking the 'no religion' box. The only apparent exception to the trend is 1996/2001, where there were significant jumps in both 'not stated' and 'inadequate description'.

Even at the time that he published, the historical census data seemed to count strongly against Bouma's prediction that *religion* would gain the attention and commitment of more in the immediate future; with the benefit of hindsight, we can see that his prediction was wrong for the immediately following years, and we can also say that there is no reason to think that his prediction will be vindicated any time soon. It is not so clear what to say about Bouma's prediction that *spirituality* would gain the attention and commitment of more in the immediate future. Since Bouma (2006: 12) tells us that 'spiritual' refers to 'an experiential journey of encounter and relationship with otherness, with powers and forces beyond the scope of everyday life', we might reasonably surmise that atheists, agnostics, humanists, and rationalists are not spiritual. But the census data doesn't tell us whether the rest of those who fall under 'no religion' or 'not stated' or 'inadequate description' are spiritual. Following Bouma's own advice, it might be that we do best not to speculate further.

Of course, that the data does not bear out Bouma's claims about growth in the proportion of those who claim religion and spirituality does not mean that the data contradicts Bouma's claims about the 'continued vitality' of religious and spiritual life in

Table 7.3 Lack of religious identification, Australia, 2006–2016

Year	No religion	Not stated/inade-quate description	Total
2006	18.7	11.9	30.6
2011	22.3	9.4	31.7
2016	30.1	10.0	40.1

Australia. One important consideration is to look at the total population at each of the census dates (Table 7.4). Even though 96.7 per cent of the population was religious in 1911, and only 69.4 per cent of the population was religious in 2016, there were 4.278 million religious people in 1911, and 16.746 million religious people in 2016. Moreover, there has been a steady growth in the absolute number of religious people across all of the census periods. There is no doubt that religion will continue to be a significant consideration in social policy for the foreseeable future.

Like McGrath, Bouma also provides theoretical considerations to buttress his empirical arguments. On the one hand, he claims that increasing diversity and the rise of faith-based schools will spawn a generation of religiously articulate youth. And, on the other hand, he claims that religion and spirituality are 'core to humanity'. However, the census data suggests that his 'generation of religiously articulate youth' will form a declining proportion of the total population. And Bouma's claims about the centrality of religion and spirituality are evidently contentious. Bouma writes:

> Secularists and anticlericals ... [insist that] ... the mature human stands before the emptiness of space and experiences neither awe nor a sense of wonder, just a non-responsive void ... [A]n uncaring and unresponsive universe provides little foundation for care for self, other, society, or environment.

But, in fact, many secularists and anti-clericals do think that awe and wonder are appropriate responses to our universe; Dawkins (2006: 11) correctly observes that 'a quasi-mystical response to nature and the universe is common among scientists and rationalists'. Moreover, most secularists and anti-clericals value care for self,

Table 7.4 Total Australian population (millions), 1911–2016

1911	1922	1933	1947	1954	1961	1966	1971	1976
4.425	5.510	6.603	7.517	8.902	10.391	11.505	12.663	13.892
1981	1986	1991	1996	2001	2006	2011	2016	
14.695	15.788	17.065	18.071	19.153	20.394	22.340	24.130	

others, society and environment, while not accepting the idea that such care is grounded in some kind of response to the emptiness of space.

In short: Bouma (2006) offers no serious support for the claim that religion and spirituality are on the rise in Australia. The relevant empirical data seems to suggest that rejection of religion and spirituality in Australia is accelerating. And the theoretical considerations to which Bouma appeals are based in crude caricatures of the views of 'secularists and anticlericals'. As we saw in the case of McGrath, Bouma's argument is driven almost exclusively by ideological commitment and wishful thinking.

7.2.4 CONCLUDING REMARKS

During the past couple of centuries, there have been many intellectuals and academics who have claimed that religion is in terminal decline. It is not at all clear that those intellectuals and academics are correct. The relevant empirical data is mixed: while there is evidence of decline of religion in the West, there is no clear evidence of decline of religion in much of the rest of the world. Moreover, the relevant theoretical considerations are contested: there is no scholarly agreement about the nature and value of religion and religious belief. However, I think that we can be quite confident that recent academic claims—in philosophy, theology and sociology—about a resurgence of religion in the West are unfounded: we do not currently possess any good empirical or theoretical reasons for thinking that the century-long decline of religion in the West is about to be reversed. Of course, this is not to say that such a reversal is ruled out; it is one thing to have lack good empirical or theoretical reasons for believing a hypothesis, and quite another to have good empirical or theoretical reasons to rule it out. However, a serious weighing of the future of atheism should proceed independently of the doctrinal commitments of those making the assessment.

7.3 THE PERILS OF PREDICTION

When we ask about the future of atheism, we are thinking about the distribution of atheistic belief among human beings. Thus, there is no adequate discussion of the future of atheism that does not consider the wider future of humanity.

What does the very long-term future hold for humanity? Well, setting aside the most bizarre and fantastic speculations, the answer to this question is straightforward: *extinction*. At some point in the future of the universe, it will no longer contain human beings, or other kinds of intelligent agents, and so there will no longer be atheists, or theists, or agnostics, or innocents. On all plausible scenarios, the universe will eventually reach a point at which it no longer contains protons and neutrons; at that point, bizarre and fantastic speculations aside, the universe will not contain human beings or any kinds of intelligent agents.

Of course, the point at which universe no longer contains protons and neutrons is many billions of years into the future; it is highly likely that humanity and intelligent agents will have disappeared from the universe long before the decay of protons and neutrons. The earth and the sun are about 4.5 billion years old. If no other catastrophe occurs, then the earth is potentially hospitable to life for another 2 billion years. Even if we find ways to leave the earth and take up residence in other parts of the universe, luminous stars will disappear from the universe in less than 200 trillion years. Setting bizarre and fantastic speculations aside, there will be no human beings or other intelligent agents in the universe when there are no more luminous stars.

While it is not hard to arrive at plausible potential upper bounds on the existence of humanity and other intelligent agents, it is much harder to arrive at plausible guesses about exactly when humanity and other intelligent agents will become extinct. In recent times, there are many writers who have made very gloomy estimates. For example, Rees (2003) thinks that it is only 50/50 that humanity will survive the twenty-first century. Whatever you think of these gloomy estimates, it is clear that there are many serious threats to the continuing existence of humanity to take into account: global warming, global degradation of arable soils, global atmospheric pollution, global exhaustion of critical resources (e.g. oil, gas, timber, rare earth metals), global extinction of insects, global extinction of marine life, global agricultural failure, global nuclear war, global biological war, global nano-technological war, failure of global financial markets, and so forth. It is not out of the question that there is not much future time in which human beings will be around to debate religion and spirituality.

Given these uncertainties about even the medium term future, it seems that we need to turn our attention to much shorter time frames. Instead of asking about what will be the case in a hundred, or a thousand, or a million, or a billion years, let's consider what will be the case in five, or ten, or twenty or fifty years. What will be the global standing of atheism in five, or ten, or twenty, or fifty years? What will be the standing of atheism in prosperous democracies in five, or ten, or twenty, or fifty years? What will be the standing of atheism in Australia, or Denmark, or France, or Germany, or Italy, or Japan, or New Zealand, or Spain, or the UK, or the US, in five, or ten, or twenty, or fifty years?

The obvious—banal—answer to these questions is that we don't know. Predicting the future is a mug's game. Even for relatively autonomous systems, such as weather, for which we have enormous data sets and complex models that contain millions of parameters, we can only make accurate predictions for somewhere between a few hours and a few days ahead. While we have an enormous amount of data, and a large array of complex models, that confirms that our planet is warming as a result of a range of factors including greenhouse gas emissions, we are unable to give a very precise estimate of how much hotter the planet will be fifty years from now. And, unsurprisingly, when it comes to the future of atheism over the next five, or ten, or twenty, or fifty years, we simply do not have big-data-backed models that yield even moderately precise predictions.

Perhaps we might be tempted to say something like this: given the currently observed correlations between religiosity and gross domestic product per capita, it is reasonable to suppose that the immediate future of atheism is tied to the immediate future of gross domestic product per capita. Where gross domestic product per capita increases, we can expect to see atheism making gains; and, perhaps, where gross domestic product per capita decreases, we can expect to see atheism losing market share. If we suppose that there will be *global* increase in gross domestic product per capita, then we might predict that we shall see a *global* increase in atheism; if we suppose that there will be global economic turmoil—perhaps because of growing shortages of key resources—

then we might predict that we shall see a global decrease in atheism. Moreover, where we suppose that there will be *local* increase in gross domestic product per capita, we might predict that we shall see *local* increase in atheism; and where we suppose that there will be local decrease in gross domestic product per capita, we might predict that we shall see local decrease in atheism.

But, of course, even if we accept that the immediate future of atheism is tied to the immediate future of gross domestic product per capita, that still leaves us with questions about the immediate future of gross domestic product per capita. Will there be local increases of gross domestic product per capita over the next five, or ten, or twenty, or fifty years? Will there be global increases of gross domestic product per capita over the next five, or ten, or twenty, or fifty years? There are many considerations—about environmental change, technological development, political decision, demographic shift, and so forth—that feed into the answers to these questions. Some, looking at considerations about peak oil, soil loss, species extinction, human population increase, air pollution, decline of water quality, income inequality, political polarisation, global warming, and the like, may be pessimistic about the prospects for continuing local and global increases in gross domestic product per capita over the next five, or ten, or twenty, or fifty years. Others, looking at the past history of pessimistic prediction, and the ways in which technological and social innovation has so far averted catastrophe, may be more optimistic about the prospects for continuing local and global increases in gross domestic product per capita over the next five, or ten, or twenty, or fifty years. Once we factor in our uncertainty about whether the immediate future of atheism is tied to the immediate future of gross domestic product per capita, we seem to be driven back to a confession of ignorance: we just don't know enough to be confident about what the future of atheism will be.

Perhaps because I'm not inclined to think that doom is absolutely imminent, I'm inclined to think that, at least in what are currently prosperous democracies, it is likely that atheism will continue to gain market share in the immediate future; it would be quite surprising to me if, in the next five or ten years, we see a sudden downturn in the numbers of atheists in Australia, and Denmark, and France, and Germany, and Italy, and Japan, and

New Zealand, and Spain, and the UK, and the US. But, in the tide of human affairs, things can change very quickly. I expect that some of us shall see.

As we noted in our discussion of McGrath (2004) and Bouma (2006), many discussions of the future of atheism fail to disentangle empirical and normative considerations. In this section, to this point, I have been considering whether we have *data* and *modelling* that supports predictions about the likely distribution of atheists in five, or ten, or twenty, or fifty years, and I have been arguing for a negative conclusion. But—as the examples of McGrath (2004) and Bouma (2006) indicate—there are many authors who make very confident predictions about the imminent demise of atheism. Why is this?

Here is my best guess. Suppose that you think that atheism is irrational, immoral, unliveable, and so on. Given your views, it is unsurprising that you think that future people *should not* be atheists. Suppose, further, that you have an optimistic outlook about the future: you think that it is unduly pessimistic to suppose that the future will be no better than the present. If you suppose that one of the ways in which the future will be better than the present is that people will generally do better in believing as they ought, then it seems to follow from the various things that you believe that it is likely that there will be fewer atheists in the future.

Of course, there are many atheists who have made confident predictions about the imminent demise of theism. I have a similar guess to make about them. Suppose that you think that theism is irrational, immoral, unliveable, and so on. Given your views, it is unsurprising that you think that future people *should not* be theists. Suppose, further, that you have an optimistic view about the future: you think that it is unduly pessimistic to suppose that the future will be no better than the present. If you suppose that one of the ways in which the future will be better than the present is that people will generally do better in believing as they ought, then it seems to follow from the various things that you believe that it is likely that there will be fewer theists in the future.

I think that the obvious response to make to both of these arguments is to deny the foundational thought. It simply isn't true that theism is irrational, immoral and unliveable; it simply isn't true that atheism is irrational, immoral and unliveable. I'm happy enough to take an optimistic view of the future: if all goes well, then people will generally do better in believing as they ought. But what this means is only that, if all goes well, people will generally do better in co-ordinating their beliefs to universal expert consensus, where there is such universal expert consensus. In areas—such as philosophy, politics, and religion—where there is clearly no universal expert consensus, there just isn't anything that people *ought* to believe; hence, in particular, in these areas, where there is a significant body of expert acceptance of a given set of beliefs, it simply isn't credible to suppose that it is irrational, or immoral, or unliveable to accept that set of beliefs.

7.4 CONCLUDING OBSERVATIONS

The upshot of my discussion of the likely future of atheism is, I suspect, disappointingly deflationary. Despite all the heat and noise, the success of the 'new' atheists is not particularly strong evidence that atheism is currently booming. Despite all the heat and noise, recent academic claims about the imminent demise of atheism are even weaker evidence that atheism is not currently booming. When we think seriously about the matter, we see that it is very hard to say, with any confidence, how atheism will fare in even the short-to-medium-term future.

WHAT TO READ NEXT

There is an enormous literature on atheism, some of which is listed in the bibliography. From the items that I have listed there, here is a 'top twenty' of things that you might like to read next. Of course, what you want to read will depend on your particular interests; the list that follows reflects the kinds of things in which I have most interest. My list is alphabetical; it is not organised according to any notion of merit.

Ali (2008)
Atran (2002)
Berman (1988)
Blackford and Schuklenk (2013)
Blom (2010)
Bonett (2010)
Budd (1977)
Christina (2016)
Flynn (2007)
Gage (1893)
Goldman (1931)
Hecht (2003)
Hunsberger and Altemeyer (2006)
Jacoby (2005)
Kaminer (2000)
Kors (1976)
McAnulla et al. (2017)
Meslier (1729/2009)
Oppy (2018)
Zuckerman (2008)

GLOSSARY OF KEY TERMS

Agnosticism Suspension of judgment about whether there are gods. An agnostic neither believes that there is at least one god nor believes that there are no gods.

Altruism Concern for welfare of others that is not grounded merely in regard for self.

Anarchism Opposition to all forms of government. An anarchist believes that voluntary co-operation should everywhere replace state coercion and persuasion.

Argument A collection of sentences—or statements, or beliefs—one of which is distinguished as the conclusion, and the rest of which are the premises.

Asceticism Abstinence and austerity. An ascetic avoids pleasure, typically in pursuit of religious goals.

Atheism The claim that there are no gods. An atheist believes that there are no gods.

Bayesian Giving pride of place to Bayes's theorem. See: https://plato.stanford.edu/entries/bayes-theorem/

Belief What is attributed to subjects by sentences of the form 'A believes that S'.

Big picture The logical closure of a logically consistent set of beliefs. Competing big pictures partition into data and worldview.

Burden of proof In a formal debate, the standard to be met by of those on the affirmative side. It is controversial whether burdens of proof arise in informal debates.

Communism Socioeconomic system centred on communal ownership of natural resources, communal ownership of major means of production, communal government and communal living.

Conclusion   In an argument, the conclusion is the sentence—statement, claim, belief—that is said to follow from the premises. For example, in the following syllogism—Socrates is Greek, all Greeks are mortal, therefore Socrates is mortal—the conclusion is that Socrates is mortal.

Conditional   A sentence of the following form: if A then B. For example, the following sentence is a conditional: if Marxists are atheists, then Marxists hate God. In the conditional if A then B, A is the antecedent and B is the consequent of that conditional.

Conservative   Ideologically opposed to change. Conservatives favour tradition, hierarchy, paternalism, subservient underclasses, and small government.

Contradiction   A sentence—statement, claim, belief—of the following form: A and not-A. For example: Trump is a good president and Trump is not a good president.

Data   In the context of comparison of big pictures, that which is common to competing big pictures, and hence, that which is to be explained by competing big pictures.

Deconstruction   A controversial method of textual analysis that focuses on ways in which 'grand narratives' and 'universalist ideologies' are undone by their own presuppositions and frames of reference.

Derivation   A series of steps that takes you from the premises of an argument to its conclusion, where each of the steps is justified by its being an application of a rule of logic.

Diachronic   Extending over time. A diachronic view considers how things change over time, whereas a synchronic view considers how things are at a particular moment in time.

Dogmatism   Imperviousness to evidence and the opinions of others. Dogmatists take their beliefs to be above question and not in need of justification.

Ethical egoism   The view that rationality requires maximisation of self-interest.

Evidence   Available information and facts. Access to evidence may require specialist training; evidence need not be obvious to all.

Explanation   Reasons or justifications. The objects of explanation are many and various: actions, events, beliefs, states, conditions, and so on.

Fascism   Radical authoritarian nationalism. Fascists are typically anti-egalitarian, opposed to freedom of expression, in love with military symbolism, and full of hate for minorities, 'deviants' and 'degenerates'.

Freethought   Valorisation of evidence and reason above authority, tradition and dogma.

Fundamentalism   Strict literalism in the interpretation of religious texts. Fundamentalists often mark in group / out group distinctions with appeals to ideals of purity and conservative yearnings for past glories that have become lost to more recent generations.

Gerrymander   Deliberate manipulation of data to fit favoured conclusions.

God   Sufficiently highly ranked supernatural being that has and exercises power over the natural universe.

Hedonism   Pursuit of one's own pleasure as one's ultimate good. Hedonists vary in their conceptions of pleasure; not all hedonists suppose that pleasure is merely sensual pleasure.

Humanism   Taking human matters to have ultimate and supreme significance. Humanists suppose that human matters are more important than supernatural and divine matters.

Ideology   Stock of fundamental or primitive ideas. The ideology of a theory is the stock of primitive predicates that are required for the formulation of the theory.

Innocence   State of never having considered whether there are gods. Innocents typically lack the idea or concept that is expressed with the word 'god'.

Knowledge   What is attributed to subjects by sentences of the form 'A knows that S'. Many philosophers have supposed that knowledge is warranted true belief: A knows that S if and only if it is true that S, and A believes that S, and A is warranted in believing that S.

Logic   Study of the relation of logical consequence and the underlying notion of logical form.

Logical closure   A set of sentences is logically closed if and only if every logical consequence of members of S is itself a member of S. The logical closure of a set of sentences S is obtained from S by adding everything that is a logical consequence of members of S to S.

Marxism   The political, economic and philosophical theories of Marx and Engels, and later theories inspired by them.

Material conditional   A conditional if A then B that is false if and only if the antecedent (A) is true and the consequent (B) is false. It is controversial whether there are material conditionals in ordinary language.

Materialism   There are none but material causal entities with none but material causal powers, and well-established science is our touchstone for identifying causal entities and causal powers. Seventeenth century materialists believed that fundamental causal entities are material atoms that interact by contact.

Meaning   That which makes sounds and inscriptions into items of communication and understanding.

Meaningless   That which merely appears to belong to the class of sounds and inscriptions that are items of communication and understanding.

Metaphysics   Philosophical inquiry that raises questions about what lies beyond or behind the domains that are studied in physics, or in the natural and human sciences.

Modus ponens   The rule of logic that say that the consequent of a conditional is a logical consequence of the conditional and its antecedent: B is a logical consequence of A and if A then B.

Monotheism   There is exactly one god: God. Some monotheists deny that God is a god; but most monotheists are happy with the claim that God is the one and only god.

Naturalism   There are none but natural causal entities with none but natural causal powers, and well-established science is our touchstone for identifying causal entities and causal powers. Some who call themselves 'naturalists' accept only the first, or only the second, part of this definition.

Negation   What is expressed by the words 'it is not the case that'. Given a sentence—statement, claim, belief—A, we express its negation as '~A'. In classical logic, ~A is true if and only if A is false.

Nihilism   Believing nothing and/or valuing nothing and/or having no allegiances and/or having no purposes. Most often, nihilists claim that nothing has any value.

Omnipotence   Traditional divine attribute. Roughly, something is omnipotent if and only if nothing could be more powerful than it.

Ontology   The branch of metaphysics that is concerned with establishing what exists. The ontology of a theory is roughly what would exist if things were as the theory says that they are.

Particularism   There are no general principles. For example, according to moral particularists, there are no general moral principles.

Philosophy   The theoretical discipline whose subject matter is those claims for which we do not have, and do not see how we might come to have, expert agreement on the methods to be used in settling their truth or falsity.

Physicalism   There are none but physical causal entities with none but physical causal powers, and well-established science is our touchstone for identifying causal entities and causal powers.

Polytheism   There is more than one god.

Postmodernism   An intellectual movement that yields a negative—sceptical, ironic—assessment of 'grand narratives' and 'universalist ideologies' and promotes a tendency towards relativist and pluralist construals of truth and knowledge.

Practical reason   Any reasoning that is aimed at determining how one—or we—should act.

Pragmatism   Roughly: the meaning of a claim is the practical effects that follow from its adoption. Pragmatists suppose that what justifies beliefs is whether they work.

Premise   One among the claims from which the conclusion of an argument is derived. In the following argument—Socrates is Greek, all Greeks are mortal, therefore Socrates is mortal—there are two premises: that Socrates is Greek and that all Greeks are mortal.

Presumption   A standard or standing presupposition.

Presupposition   Something that is taken for granted. When reasoning is not made fully explicit, it often contains hidden presuppositions.

Proof   A correct derivation from premises universally accepted by relevant experts.

Rationalism   Emphasis on the central role that reason plays in the acquisition and justification of knowledge. More broadly, rationalists are anti-clerical humanists.

Rationality   Capacity to revise and update arguments, behaviour, beliefs, institutions, policies and practices in the light of new information.

Religion   Passionate communal display of costly material commitments to appropriate entities thereby enabling mastery of existential anxieties under ritualised rhythmic sensory coordination in congregation and fellowship.

Religiosity   Strong religious feeling or belief.

Sceptic   One who claims that there is very little that we are rationally justified in believing about the external world, other minds, the extent of the past, morality, modality, meaning, and so forth. Scepticism typically requires suspension of judgment about almost everything.

Secular   Concerned with the natural world, rather than with sacred, or ecclesiastical, or monastic matters. Secularists maintain that the sacred, and the ecclesiastical, and the monastic should be strictly confined to private domains.

Socialism   Socio-economic system in which means of production are under social control. Differs from communism by working within liberal democratic constitutions.

Sound   An argument is sound if and only it is valid and possessed of true premises. The following argument—Socrates is Greek, all Greeks are mortal, therefore Socrates is mortal—is sound.

Spirituality   A sense of connection to something above or beyond natural causal reality. It is currently quite common for people to claim to be spiritual but not religious.

Synchronic   Concerned with how things are at a particular moment in time.

Tautology   A (formal) logical truth. Example: All red things are red. According to some, all tautologies are trivial.

Theology   Systematic study of gods. Typically conducted by theists, that is, by those who believe that there is at least one god.

Theoretical commitment   What someone who accepts a given theory is committed to by that theory. Theoretical commitments may be ontological and/or ideological and/or nomological.

Theoretical reason Any reasoning that is aimed at determining what to believe.

Theoretical virtue Whatever it is that makes one theory better than another. One common view is that greater theoretical virtue is a matter of making the best trade-off between minimising theoretical commitment and maximising explanatory breadth and depth.

Theory A set of claims about a given subject matter. In principle, theories can aim to give comprehensive treatments of given subject matters.

Valid An argument is valid just in case its conclusion is a logical consequence of its premises. Validity is a sine qua non for derivation.

Worldview In the context of comparison of big pictures, that which differs between competing big pictures.

BIBLIOGRAPHY

Addley, S. (2013) 'Atheist Sunday Assembly Branches Out in First Wave of Expansion', *The Guardian*, 14 September, www.theguardian.com/world/2013/sep/14/atheist-sunday-assembly-branches-out

AFP (2016) 'The Lonesome Life of Africa's Atheists', *Daily Nation*, www.nation.co.ke/lifestyle/The-lonesome-life-of-Africa-atheists-GHANA/1190-3497954-3ud5qmz/index.html

Ali, A. (2008) *Infidel*, New York: Atria

Al-Ma'arri, A. (2016) *The Epistle of Forgiveness*, edited and translated by G. van Gelder and G. Schoeler, New York: New York University Press

Angier, N. (2004) 'My God Problem—and Theirs', *Edge*www.edge.org/conversation/natalie_angier-my-god-problem

Atambire, A. (2014) 'My Visit to a Traditional African Priest', *GhanaWeb*, www.ghanaweb.com/GhanaHomePage/features//My-Visit-to-a-Traditional-African-Priest-314976

Atambire, A. (2016) 'Saying NO GMO Won't Make it Go Away', *Harmattangh.com*, http://harmattangh.com/feature-saying-no-gmo-wont-make-it-go-away/

Atambire, A. (2017a) 'The Misplaced Priority of Food Sovereignty in the GMO Debate', *Graphic.com*, www.graphic.com.gh/business/business-news/the-misplaced-priority-of-food-sovereignty-on-the-gmos-debate.html

Atambire, A. (2017b) 'Solidarity without a Power Shift?', *The Summit of Colonialism?*, https://issuu.com/dshamiljaroshani/docs/der_gipfel_des_kolonialismus-

Atran, S. (2002) *In Gods we Trust: The Evolutionary Landscape of Religion*, Oxford: Oxford University Press

Ayer, A. J. (1936) *Language Truth and Logic*, London: Gollancz

Bainbridge, W. (2005) 'Atheism', *Interdisciplinary Journal of Research on Religion* 1/2: 1–26

Barnett, A. and Namazie, M. (2011) *Enemies not Allies: The Far Right*, London: One Law for All

Beit-Hallahmi, B. (2007) 'Atheists: A Psychological Profile', in M. Martin (ed.) *The Cambridge Companion to Atheism*, Cambridge: Cambridge University Press, 300–317

Bekiempis, V. (2011) 'New Atheism and the Old Boys Club', *BitchMedia*, www.bitchmedia.org/article/the-unbelievers

Berman, D. (1988) *A History of Atheism in Great Britain*, London: Routledge

Bhattacharya, R. (2011) *Studies in Cārvāka/Lokāyata*, London: Anthem Press

Blackford, R. and Schuklenk, U. (2013) *Fifty Great Myths about Atheism*, Oxford: Wiley-Blackwell

Blom, P. (2010) *A Wicked Company: The Forgotten Radicalism of the European Enlightenment*, New York: Basic Books

Bonett, W. (ed.) (2010) *The Australian Book of Atheism*, Melbourne: Scribe

Bouma, G. (2006) *Australian Soul: Religion and Spirituality in the Twenty-First Century*, Melbourne: Cambridge University Press

Bremmer, J. (2007) 'Atheism in Antiquity', in M. Martin (ed.) *The Cambridge Companion to Atheism*, Cambridge: Cambridge University Press, 11–26

Brown, C. (2012) '"The Unholy Mrs. Knight" and the BBC', *OUPblog*, https://blog.oup.com/2012/05/unholy-mrs-knight-bbc/

Bruce, S. (2002) *God is Dead: Secularisation in the West*, Oxford: Blackwell

Budd, S. (1977) *Varieties of Unbelief: Atheists and Agnostics in English Society 1850–1960*, Portsmouth: Heinemann

Bukharin, N. and Preobrazhensky, R. (1920/1969) *The ABC of Communism*, Harmondsworth: Penguin

Bullivant, S. and Ruse, M. (eds) (2013) *The Oxford Handbook of Atheism*, Oxford: Oxford University Press

Caldwell-Harris, C. *et al.* (2017) 'Exploring the Atheist Personality: Well-Being, Awe, and Magical Thinking in Atheists, Buddhists, and Christians', *Mental Health, Religion and Culture* 14: 659–672

CFI (2017) 'Al Ma'arri', www.centerforinquiry.net/secularislam/islamic_viewpoints/al_maarri/

Chattopadhyaya, D. (1959) *Lokāyata: A Study in Ancient Indian Materialism*, New Delhi: People's Publishing House

Christina, G. (2016) *The Way of the Heathen: Practising Atheism in Everyday Life*, Durham: Pitchstone Publishing

Cohen, C. (1921) *Theism or Atheism*, London: Pioneer Press

Craig, W. (undated) 'The Revolution in Anglo-American Philosophy', *Reasonable Faith*, www.reasonablefaith.org/writings/popular-writings/apologetics/the-revolution-in-anglo-american-philosophy/

Craig, W. and Moreland, J. (2009) *The Blackwell Companion to Natural Theology*, Malden, MA: Wiley-Blackwell

Curlin, F. *et al.* (2005) 'Religious Characteristics of US Physicians: A National Survey', *Journal of General Internal Medicine* 20: 629–634

Curran, M. (2012) *Atheism, Religion and Enlightenment in Pre-Revolutionary Europe*, London: Boydell & Brewer

Cushing, M. (1914) *Baron d'Holbach: A Study of Eighteenth Century Radicalism in France*, New York: Columbia University Press

Dawkins, R. (2004) *A Devil's Chaplain: Reflections on Hope, Lies, Science and Love*, New York: Houghton Mifflin Harcourt

Dawkins, R. (2006) *The God Delusion* London: Bantam Press

Decety, J. *et al.* (2015) 'The Negative Association between Religiousness and Children's Altruism across the World', *Current Biology* 25: 2951–2955

Dennett, D. (2006) *Breaking the Spell: Religion as a Natural Phenomenon*, London: Allen Lane

Drum, K. (2017) 'Atheists Open Gap against Muslims for Title of most Hated Religious Group in America', *Mother Jones*, www.motherjones.com/kevin-drum/2017/02/atheists-no-longer-most-hated-religious-group-america/

Ecklund, E. and Scheitle, C. (2007) 'Religion and Academic Scientists: Distinctions, Disciplines and Demographics', *Social Problems* 54: 289–307

Ecklund, E., *et al.* (2016) 'Religion among Scientists in International Context: A New Study of Scientists in Eight Regions', *Socius* 2: 1–9

Edelman, B. (2009) 'Red Light States: Who Buys On-Line Adult Entertainment?', *Journal of Economic Perspectives* 23: 209–220

Edgell, P., Gerteis, J. and Hartmann, D. (2006) 'Atheists as "Other": Moral Boundaries and Cultural Membership in American Society', *American Sociological Review* 71: 211–234

Egnor, M. (2007) 'Atheistic Fundamentalism and the Limits of Science', *Evolution News*, https://evolutionnews.org/2007/10/fundamentalism_and_dr_forrest/

Exline, J. *et al.* (2011) 'Anger toward God: Social-Cognitive Predictors, Prevalence, and Links with Adjustment to Bereavement and Cancer', *Journal of Personality and Social Psychology* 100: 129–148

Filonik, J. (2013) 'Athenian Impiety Trials: A Reappraisal', *Dike* 16: 11–96

Flynn, T. (ed.) (2007) *The New Encyclopedia of Unbelief* Amherst, MA: Prometheus

Flynn, T. (2012) 'Why I Don't Believe in the New Atheism', www.secularhumanism.org/index.php?section=library&page=flynn_30_3

Foote, G. (1886) *Prisoner for Blasphemy* London: Progressive Publishing Co.

Frazier, J. (2013) 'Hinduism', in S. Bullivant and M. Ruse (eds), *The Oxford Handbook of Atheism* Oxford: Oxford University Press, 367–379

Fuller, R. (2001) *Spiritual but not Religious: Understanding Unchurched America* New York: Oxford University Press

Gage, M. (1893) *Woman, Church and State* New York: Truth Seeker Co.

Gervais, W. and Najile, M. (2017) 'How Many Atheists Are There?', *Social Psychological and Personality Science*, doi:10.1177/1948550617707015

Gervais, W., Norenzayan, A. and Shariff, A. (2011) 'Do you Believe in Atheists? Distrust is Central to Anti-Atheist Prejudice', *Journal of Personality and Social Psychology* 101: 1189–1206

Gervais, W. *et al.* (2017) 'Global Evidence of Extreme Intuitive Moral Prejudice against Atheists', *Nature Human Behaviour Letters* 1: 1–5

Goldberg, M. (2007) *Kingdom Coming: The Rise of Christian Nationalism*, New York: W. W. Norton

Goldman, E.(1908) 'What I Believe', *New York World*, 19 July, reprinted at http s://babel.hathitrust.org/cgi/pt?id=mdp.39015081787973;view=1up;seq=9

Goldman, E. (1923) 'Oftener Brief an den Herausgeber der Jahrbücher über Louise Michel', with a preface by Magnus Hirschfeld, *Jahrbuch für sexuelle Zwischenstufen* 23, www.angelfire.com/ok/Flack/emma.html

Goldman, E. (1931) *Living my Life*, New York: Knopf

Goldstein, R. (2011) *36 Arguments for the Existence of God: A Work of Fiction*, New York: Vintage

Grayling, A. (2007) *Against All Gods: Six Polemics on Religion and an Essay on Kindness*, London: Oberon Books

Gross, N. and Simmons, S. (2009) 'The Religiosity of American College and University Professors', *Sociology of Religion* 70: 101–129

Hackney, C. and Sanders, G. (2003) 'Religiosity and Mental Health: A Meta-Analysis of Recent Studies', *Journal for the Scientific Study of Religion* 42: 43–56

Haldeman-Julius, E. (1926) *The Militant Agnostic*, Girard: Haldeman-Julius Publications

Haley, K. and Fessler, D. (2005) 'Nobody's Watching? Subtle Cues Affect Generosity in an Anonymous Economic Game', *Evolution and Human Behaviour* 26: 245–256

Hall, D. (2010) 'Why Don't We Practice What We Preach? A Meta-Analytic View of Religious Racism', *Personality and Social Psychology Review* 14: 126–139

Harper, M. (2007) 'The Stereotyping of Non-Religious People by Religious Students: Contents and Subtypes', *Journal for the Scientific Study of Religion* 46: 539–552

Harris, S. (2004) *The End of Faith: Religion, Terror, and the Future of Reason*, New York: W. W. Norton

Hayward, R.*et al.* (2016) 'Health and Well-Being among the Non-Religious: Atheists, Agnostics, and No Preference Compared with Religious Group Members', *Journal of Religion and Health* 55: 1024–1037

Hecht, J. (2003) *Doubt: A History*, San Francisco, CA: HarperOne

Hitchens, C. (2007) *God is not Great: How Religion Poisons Everything*, New York: Allen & Unwin

Holbach, P. (1772/1900) *Good Sense without God*, London: W. Stewart & Co

Hoskin, A. *et al.* (2017) 'Does Religiosity Explain Cross-National Differences in Crime: The Case of American versus Malaysian University Students', *Journal of Religion and Society* 19: 1–16

Hughes, K. (1998) *George Eliot: The Last Victorian*, New York: Farrar, Straus & Giroux

Hunsberger, E. and Altemeyer, B. (2006) *Atheists: A Ground-Breaking Study of America's Non-Believers*, Amherst, MA: Prometheus

Hunter, M. and Wootton, D. (eds) (1992) *Atheism from the Reformation to the Enlightenment*, Oxford: Clarendon

Hustinx, L.*et al.* (2015) 'A Cross-National Examination of the Motivation to Volunteer: Religious Context, National Value Patterns, and Non-Profit Regimes', in L. Hustinx et al. (eds), *Religion and Volunteering*, Zurich: Springer, 97–120

Hwang, K., Hammer, J. and Cragun, R. (2011) 'Extending Religion-Health Research to Secular Minorities: Issues and Concerns', *Journal of Religion and Health* 50: 608–622

Ingersoll, R. (1872) *The Gods*, http://infidels.org/library/historical/robert_ingersoll/gods.html

Jacobsen, S. (2016) 'Extended Interview with Maryam Namazie, Iranian-Born Secularist and Human Rights Activist', *Europe Solidaire sans Frontières*, www.europe-solidaire.org/spip.php?article39206

Jacoby, S. (2005) *Freethinkers: A History of American Secularism*, New York: Holt

Ji, C., Pendergraft, L. and Perry, M. (2006) 'Religiosity, Altruism, and Altruistic Hypocrisy: Evidence from Protestant Adolescents', *Review of Religious Research* 48: 156–178

Jim, H. *et al.* (2015) 'Religion, Spirituality and Physical Health in Cancer Patients', *Cancer* 121: 3760–3768

Jinn, B. (2013) *Illogical Atheism*, [no location]: Divided Line

Jong, J. and Halberstadt, J. (2016) *Death Anxiety and Religious Belief: An Existential Psychology of Religion*, London: Bloomsbury

Jong, J. and Halberstadt, J. (2018) 'Death Anxiety and Religious Belief: Response to Commentaries' *Religion, Brain and Behaviour*, doi:10.1080/2153599X.2017.1414712

Kahneman, D. (2011) *Thinking Fast and Slow*, New York: Farrar, Straus & Giroux

Kamel, M. (2015) 'The 11th Century Poet Who Pissed Off al-Qaeda', *History Answers*, www.historyanswers.co.uk/medieval-renaissance/al-maarri-the-11th-century-poet-that-pissed-off-al-qaeda/

Kaminer, W. (2000) *Sleeping with Extra-Terrestrials: The Rise of Irrationalism and the Perils of Piety*, New York: Vintage

Kanazawa, S. (2010) 'Why Liberals and Atheists are More Intelligent', *Social Psychological Quarterly* 73: 33–57

Kettell, S. (2013) 'Faithless: The Politics of New Atheism', *Secularity and Non-Religion* 2: 61–78

Keysar, A. (2007) 'Who are America's Atheists and Agnostics', in B. Kosmin and A. Keysar (eds), *Secularism and Secularity: Contemporary International Perspectives*, London: Transaction, 33–39

Knight, M. (1950) *William James: A Selection from his Writings on Psychology*, Harmondsworth: Penguin

Knight, M. (1955) *Morals without Religion and Other Essays*, London: Dobson

Knight, M. (ed.) (1961) *Humanist Anthology: From Confucius to Bertrand Russell*, London: Barrie & Rockliff

Knight, M. (1974) *Honest to Man: Christian Ethics Re-Examined*, London: Elek

Knight, M. and Knight, R. (1948) *A Modern Introduction to Psychology*, London: University Tutorial Press

Koenig, R. and Myers, B. (2017) 'A Mismatch between Need and Affluence', *The Chronicle of Philanthropy*, www.philanthropy.com/interactives/how-america-gives-opportunity-index

Kohut, A. et al. (2009) 'Public Praises Science; Scientists Fault Public, Media', Pew Research Centre, http://www.people-press.org/2009/07/09/public-praises-science-scientists-fault-public-media/

Kors, A. (1976) *D'Holbach's Coterie*, Princeton, NJ: Princeton University Press

Kosmin, B. and Keysar, A. (2009) 'American Religious Identification Survey (ARIS 20008)', www.americanreligionsurvey-aris.org/reports/ARIS_Report_2008.pdf

Kurtz, P. (1987) *The Transcendental Temptation*, Amherst, MA: Prometheus

Larsen, E. and Witham, L. (1998a) 'Scientists are Still Keeping the Faith', *Nature* 386: 435–436

Larsen, E. and Witham, L. (1998b) 'Leading Scientists Still Reject God', *Nature* 394: 313

LeBuffe, M. (2014) 'Paul-Henri Thiry (Baron) d'Holbach', *Stanford Encyclopedia of Philosophy*https://plato.stanford.edu/entries/holbach/

Lee, A. (2012) 'Atheism's Growing Pains', *Salon*, www.salon.com/2012/10/06/atheisms_growing_pains

Lenin, V. (1905/1954) *Socialism and Religion*, Moscow: Foreign Languages Publishing Househttp://ciml.250x.com/archive/lenin/english/lenin_1905_socialism_and_religion.pdf

Le Poidevin, R. (1996) *Arguing for Atheism: An Introduction to the Philosophy of Religion*, London: Routledge

Levin, J. and Vanderpool, H. (1991) 'Religious Factors in Physical Health and Prevention of Illness', *Prevention in Human Services* 9: 41–64

Lewis, J. (1954) *An Atheist Manifesto*, New York: Freethought Press

Lipka, M. (2016) 'US Religious Groups and their Political Leanings', Pew Research Centre, www.pewresearch.org/fact-tank/2016/02/23/u-s-religious-groups-and-their-political-leanings/

Locke, J. (1689/1983) *A Letter Concerning Toleration*, edited by J. Tully, Indianapolis: Hackett.

Lugo, L. (2010) 'US Religious Knowledge Survey', Pew Research Centre file:///C:/Users/goppy/Downloads/religious-knowledge-full-report.pdf

Lugo, L. (2012) '"Nones" on the Rise: One-in-Five have no Religious Affiliation', Pew Research Centre, www.pewforum.org/2012/10/09/nones-on-the-rise/

Lynn, R., Harvey, J. and Nyborg, H. (2009) 'Average Intelligence Predicts Atheism Rates Across 137 Nations', *Intelligence* 37: 11–15

Mackie, J. (1982) *The Miracle of Theism*, Oxford: Clarendon.

Malik, K. (2011) 'The Poetry of an Old Atheist', *Pandaemonium*, https://kenanmalik.wordpress.com/2011/04/25/old-atheist/

Martin, M. (1990) *Atheism: A Philosophical Justification*, Philadelphia, PA: Temple University Press

Martin, M. (ed.) (2007) *The Cambridge Companion to Atheism*, Cambridge: Cambridge University Press

Masters, K. and Spielmans, G. (2007) 'Prayer and Health: Meta-Analysis and Research Agenda', *Journal of Behavioural Medicine* 30: 329–338

McAnulla, S. (2012) 'Radical Atheism and Religious Power: New Atheist Politics', *Approaching Religion* 2: 87–99

McAnulla, S., Kettell, S. and Schulzke, M. (2017) *The Politics of New Atheism*, London: Routledge

McCabe, J. (1917) *The Bankruptcy of Religion*, London: Watts & Co.

McCreight, J. (2012) 'How I Unwittingly Infiltrated the Boy's Club and Why it's Time for a New Wave of Atheism', *Freethought Blogs*, https://freethoughtblogs.com/blaghag/2012/08/how-i-unwittingly-infiltrated-the-boys-club-why-its-time-for-a-new-wave-of-atheism/

McGrath, A. ((2004) *The Twilight of Atheism: The Rise and Fall of Disbelief in the Modern World*, London: Rider

McGrath, A. (2007) *The Dawkins Delusion: Atheist Fundamentalism and Denial of the Divine*, Downers Grove, IL: InterVarsity Press

Mehta, H. (2015) 'Atheists Now Make Up 0.1% of the Federal Prison Population', *Patheos*, www.patheos.com/blogs/friendlyatheist/2015/08/21/atheists-now-make-up-0-1-of-the-federal-prison-population/

Meslier, J. (1729/2009) *Testament*, translated by M. Shreve, Amherst, MA: Prometheus

Michael, R. *et al.* (1995) *Sex in America: A Definitive Survey*, New York: Warner Books

Moore, J. and Leach, M. (2016) 'Dogmatism and Mental Health: A Comparison of the Religious and the Secular', *Psychology of Religion and Spirituality* 8: 54–64

Morgan, J. (2013) 'Untangling False Assumptions Regarding Atheism and Health', *Zygon* 48: 9–19

Moritz, T. (2001) *The World's Most Dangerous Woman: A New Biography of Emma Goldman*, Vancouver: Subway Books

Nagasawa, Y. (2017) *Maximal God: A New Defence of Perfect Being Theism*, Oxford: Oxford University Press

Namazie, M. (2010) *Sharia Law in Britain: A Threat to One Law for All and Equal Rights*, London: One Law for All

Namazie, M. (undated) 'Neither Veil nor Submission' *Fitnah: Time for Change*, http://fitnah.org/fitnah_articles_english/M-namazie-nither-veil.html

Namazie, M., Mahmoud, N. and Khatiri, A. (2013) *Political and Legal Status of Apostates in Islam*, London: Council of Ex-Muslims of Britain

Nicholson, R. (1907) *A Literary History of the Arabs*, New York: Charles Scribner's Sons

Nicholson, R. (1921) *Studies in Islamic Poetry*, Cambridge: Cambridge University Press

Nietzsche, F. (1888/1976) *Twilight of the Idols*, in W. Kaufman, (ed.), *The Portable Nietzsche*, Harmondsworth: Penguin

Norris, P. and Inglehart, R. (2004) *Sacred and Secular: Religion and Politics Worldwide*, New York: Cambridge University Press

Onfray, M. (2006) 'Jean Meslier and "The Gentle Inclination of Nature"', *New Politics* X-4: 40, http://newpol.org/content/jean-meslier-and-gentle-inclination-nature

Onfray, M. (2007) *Atheist Manifesto*, translated by J. Leggatt, New York: Arcade Publishing

Oppy, G. (2013) *The Best Argument against God*, New York: Palgrave Macmillan

Oppy, G. (ed.) (2018) *The Blackwell Companion to Atheism and Philosophy*, Chichester: Wiley-Blackwell

Oppy, G. (forthcoming) 'Philosophy, Religion and Worldview' in A. Simmons (ed.) *Christian Philosophy Today and Tomorrow*, Oxford: Oxford University Press

Orwell, G. (1947) 'Lear, Tolstoy and the Fool' *Polemic* 7; reprinted in *Collected Essays*, Norwich: Martin, Secker and Warburg, 1961, 415–434

Orwell, S. and Angus, I. (eds) (1968) *The Collected Essays, Journalism and Letters of George Orwell: An Age like This, 1920–1940*, Volume 1, New York: Harcourt, Brace & World

Paine, T. (1794/1807) *The Age of Reason*, http://ebooks.adelaide.edu.au/p/paine/thomas/p147a/conclusion.html

Pargament, K. (2002) 'The Bitter and the Sweet: An Evaluation of the Costs and Benefits of Religiousness', *Psychological Inquiry* 13: 168–181

Pataki, T. (2007) *Against Religion*, Melbourne: Scribe

Paterson, J. and Francis, A. (2017) 'Influence of Religiosity on Self-Reported Response to Psychological Therapies', *Mental Health, Religion and Culture* 20: 428–448

Paul, G. (2005) 'Cross-National Correlations of Quantifiable Societal Health with Popular Religiosity and Secularism in Prosperous Democracies', *Journal of Religion and Society* 7: 1–17

Paul, G. (2009) 'The Chronic Dependence of Popular Religiosity upon Dysfunctional Psychosociological Conditions', *Evolutionary Psychology* 7: 398–441

Peterson, G. (2010) 'Ethics, Out-Group Altruism and the New Atheism', in A. Amarasingam (ed.) *Religion and the New Atheism: A Critical Appraisal*, Leiden: Brill, 159–177

Phipps, S. (2013) 'Should We Care Whether God Exists?', *Nooga.com*, http://nooga.com/164154/apatheism-should-we-care-whether-god-exists/

Powell, L., Shahabi, L. and Thoresen, C. (2003) 'Religion and Spirituality: Linkages to Physical Health', *American Psychologist* 58: 36–52

Putnam, R. (2000) *Bowling Alone: The Collapse and Revival of American Community*, New York: Touchstone

Quine, W. (1960) *Word and Object*, Cambridge, MA: MIT Press

Rauch, J. (2003) 'Let it be: Three Cheers for Apatheism', *The Atlantic Monthly*, www.theatlantic.com/magazine/archive/2003/05/let-it-be/302726/

Rees, M. (2003) *Our Final Century: Will the Human Race Survive the Twenty-First Century?*, New York: Heinemann

Rey, G. (2007) 'Meta-Atheism: Religious Avowal as Self-Deception', in L. Antony (ed.) *Philosophers without Gods: Meditations on Atheism and the Secular Life*, Oxford: Oxford University Press, 243–265

Roberts, H. (2014) 'Atheism: The New Fundamentalism?', *HuffPost*, www.huffingtonpost.com/w-hunter-roberts/atheism-the-new-fundament_b_4767900.html

Robinson, J. (1963) *Honest to God*, London: SCM Press

Rosenbaum, J. (2009) 'Patient Teenagers? A Comparison of the Sexual Behaviour of Virginity Pledgers and Matched Non-Pledgers', *Paediatrics* 123: 110–120

Ross, C. (1990) 'Religion and Psychological Distress', *Journal for the Scientific Study of Religion* 29: 236–245

Rottman, G. (2007) *Soviet Rifleman 1941–45*, London: Osprey

Russell, B. (1925) *What I Believe*, London: Kegan Paul, Trench Trübner & Co.

Russell, B. (1955) 'Promoting Virtuous Conduct', *The Observer*, 20 February; reprinted in B. Russell (2003) *Man's Peril 1954–5*, edited by A. Bone, London: Routledge, 226–231

Russell, B. (1957) *Why I Am Not a Christian*, London: Allen & Unwin

Russell, B. (2003) *Man's Peril 1954–5*, edited by A. Bone, London: Routledge

Schroeder, R., Broadus, E. and Bradley, C. (2017) 'Religiosity and Crime Revisited: Accounting for Non-Believers', *Journal of Deviant Behaviour* doi:10.1080/01639625.2017.1286183

Schulzke, M. (2013) 'The Politics of the New Atheism', *Politics and Religion* 6: 778–799

Schweizer, B. (2011) *Hating God: The Untold Story of Misotheism*, Oxford: Oxford University Press

Shariatmadari, D. (2015) 'There's Nothing Misguided about the Left's Concern for Muslims', *The Guardian*, www.theguardian.com/commentisfree/2015/oct/01/university-of-warwick-maryam-namazie-activist

Shariff, A.*et al.* (2016) 'What is the Association between Religious Affiliation and Children's Altruism?', *Current Biology* 26: R699–R700

Sheard, M. (2014) 'Ninety-Eight Atheists: Atheism among the Non-Elite in Twentieth Century Britain', *Secularism and Non-Religion*, https://secularismandnonreligion.org/articles/10.5334/snr.ar/

Sherkat, D. (2008) 'Beyond Belief: Atheism, Agnosticism and Theistic Certainty in the United States', *Sociological Spectrum* 28: 438–459

Sider, R. (2005) *The Scandal of the Evangelical Conscience: Why are Christians just like the rest of the World?*, Grand Rapids, MI: Baker

Sinnott-Armstrong, W. (2009) *Morality without God?*, Oxford: Oxford University Press

Smith, J. (2011) 'Becoming an Atheist in America: Constructing Identity and Meaning from the Rejection of Theism', *Sociology of Religion* 72: 215–237

Snyder, J. A. (undated) 'Atheism is the Philosophical Equivalent ...', www.goodreads.com/quotes/8683870-atheism-is-the-philosophical-equivalent-of-a-fish-denying-the

Sobel, J. (2004) *Logic and Theism*, Cambridge: Cambridge University Press.

Sosis, R. (2005) 'Does Religion Promote Trust? The Role of Signalling, Reputation, and Punishment', *Interdisciplinary Journal of Research on Religion* 1(7): 1–30

Sporenda, F. (2017) 'Leaving Islam: Interview with Maryam Namazie', https://revolutionfeministe.wordpress.com/2017/02/11/leaving-islam-interview-of-maryam-namazie/

Stanton, E. (1895) *The Woman's Bible*, www.gutenberg.org/ebooks/9880

Stedman, C. (2011) 'The Problem with "Atheist Activism"', *HuffPost*, www.huffingtonpost.com/chris-stedman/atheist-activism-problems_b_1164399.html

Stenger, V. (2007) *God: The Failed Hypothesis*, Amherst, MA: Prometheus

Stirrat, M. and Cornwell, E. (2013) 'Eminent Scientists Reject the Supernatural: A Survey of the Royal Society', *Evolution: Education and Outreach* 6https://link.springer.com/content/pdf/10.1186%2F1936-6434-6-33.pdf

Tan, J. and Vogel, C. (2008) 'Religion and Trust: An Experimental Study', *Journal of Economic Psychology* 29: 832–848

Taylor, D. (2003) *Orwell: The Life*, New York: Henry Holt

Thrower, J. (1980) *The Alternative Tradition: Religion and the Rejection of Religion in the Ancient World*, The Hague: Mouton

Thrower, J. (2000) *Western Atheism: A Short History*, Amherst, MA: Prometheus

Tversky, A. and Kahneman, D. (1983) 'Extension versus Intuitive Reasoning: The Conjunction Fallacy in Probabilistic Judgment', *Psychological Review* 90: 293–315

Vogt, B. (2016) 'Five Surprising Facts from the Latest US Poll about God and Atheism', https://brandonvogt.com/5-surprising-facts-latest-u-s-poll-god-a theism/

Von Hegner, I. (2016) 'Gods and Dictatorships: A Defence of Heroic Apatheism', *Science, Religion and Culture* 3: 31–48

Wang, C. (1907) *Lung Heng, Part 1, Philosophical Essays of Wang Ch'ung*, translated by A. Forke, London: Luzac

Watkin, C. (2011) *Difficult Atheism: Post-Theological Thinking in Alain Badiou, Jean-Luc Nancy and Quentin Meillassoux*, Edinburgh: Edinburgh University Press

Watson, R. (1796) *An Apology for the Bible, in a Series of Letters, Addressed to Thomas Paine, Author of a Book Entitled, The Age of Reason, Part the Second, Being an Investigation of True and Fabulous Theology*, New York: T & J Swords

Waugh, E. (1946) 'Review of Orwell's Critical Essays', *Tablet* (6 April)

Weikart, R. (2016) *Hitler's Religion: The Twisted Beliefs that Drove the Third Reich*, Washington, DC: Regnery History

Weiss, P. and Kensinger, L. (eds) (2007) *Feminist Interpretations of Emma Goldman*, Durham, NC: Duke University Press

Whitely, B. (2009) 'Religiosity and Attitudes towards Lesbians and Gay Men: A Meta-Analysis', *The International Journal for the Psychology of Religion* 19: 21–38

Whitmarsh, T. (2015) *Battling the Gods: Atheism in the Ancient World*, New York: Knopf

Wielenberg, E. (2005) *Value and Virtue in a Godless Universe*, Cambridge: Cambridge University Press

Wilde, L. (2010) 'The Antinomies of Aggressive Atheists', *Contemporary Political Theory* 9: 266–283

Winiarczyk, M. (2016) *Diagoras of Melos: A Contribution to the History of Ancient Atheism*, translated by W. Zbirohowski-Kościa, Berlin: De Gruyter

Woodbury, L. (1965) 'The Date and Atheism of Diagoras of Melos', *Phoenix* 19: 178–211

Wu, A. *et al.* (2015) 'Religion and Completed Suicide: A Meta-Analysis' *PLoS One* 10(6): e0131715

Yeghiyan, P. (1945) 'The Philosophy of Al-Ma'arri', *The Muslim World* 35: 224–236

Yirenkyi, K. and Takyi, B. (2009) 'Some Insights into Atheism and Secularity in Ghana', in P. Zuckerman (ed.) *Atheism and Secularity*, Westport, CT: Praeger vol. 2, 73–89

Zuckerman, P. (2008) *Society without God: What the Least Religious Nations can tell us about Contentment*, New York: New York University Press

Zuckerman, P. (2009a) 'Atheism, Secularity and Well-Being: How the Findings of Social Science Counter Negative Stereotypes and Assumptions', *Sociology Compass* 3: 949–971

Zuckerman, P. (ed.) (2009b) *Atheism and Secularity*, 2 volumes, Westport, CT: Praeger

INDEX